EVERY RIVER ON EARTH

EVERY RIVER ON EARTH

writing from appalachian ohio

Edited by Neil Carpathios

Foreword by Donald Ray Pollock

OHIO UNIVERSITY PRESS
ATHENS, OHIO

Ohio University Press, Athens, Ohio 45701
ohioswallow.com

Printed in the United States of America
Ohio University Press books are printed on acid-free paper ∞ ™⊗

25 24 23 22 21 20 19 18 17 16 15   5 4 3 2 1

Library of Congress Cataloging-in-Publication Data
Every river on earth : writing from Appalachian Ohio / edited by Neil Carpathios ; foreword
by Donald Ray Pollock.
    pages cm
  Summary:"*Every River on Earth: Writing from Appalachian Ohio* includes some of the best
regional poetry, fiction, and creative nonfiction from forty contemporary writers, both
established and up-and-coming. The wide range of material from authors such as David Baker,
Don Bogen, Michelle Burke, Richard Hague, Donald Ray Pollock, and others, offers the
reader a window into daily life in the region. The people, the landscape, the struggles, and the
deepest undercurrents of what it means to be from and of a place are revealed in these original,
deeply moving, and sometimes shocking pieces. The book is divided into four sections: Family
and Folks, The Land, The Grind, and Home and Away, each of which explores a different
aspect of the place that these authors call home. The sections work together beautifully to
capture what it means to live, to love, and to die in this particular slice of Appalachia. The
writing is accessible and often emotionally raw; *Every River on Earth* invites all types of readers
and conveys a profound appreciation of the region's character. The authors also offer personal
statements about their writing, allowing the reader an intimate insight into their processes,
aesthetics, and inspirations. What is it to be an Appalachian? What is it to be an Appalachian
in Ohio? This book vividly paints that picture."— Provided by publisher.
  ISBN 978-0-8214-2128-4 (hardback : acid-free paper) — ISBN 978-0-8214-2129-1 (pb) —
ISBN 978-0-8214-4510-5 (pdf)
  1. Ohio—Literary collections. 2. Appalachian Region—Literary collections. I. Carpathios,
Neil, editor.
  PS571.O3E94 2015
  810.8'09771—dc23

2014038531

CONTENTS

II. THE LAND

III. THE GRIND

IV. HOME AND AWAY

FOREWORD

I was raised in Knockemstiff in southern Ohio, and have never lived more than a few miles from that "holler" my entire life. As a teenager, I spent a major portion of my time fantasizing about being someone else somewhere else. I was unhappy for various reasons and wanted desperately to leave this place. After dropping out of high school, I hired on at the paper mill in Chillicothe where my father and grandfather worked. I had many reservations about doing that, but I was broke and told myself I'd work there just long enough to save some money, then move on to some other state, maybe Florida or California or New York. Anywhere but here in the sticks. However, that never happened. After I started working at the factory, my life quickly became complicated and messy and I married a couple of times and lived from paycheck to paycheck. When I wasn't punching the clock, I was either drinking in a bar or driving around the hills getting high in whatever old junker I could afford. I saw a lot of things during those years that would later influence my fiction, but at the time I was just trying to survive one more day without getting fired or hurting myself. Like most drunks, I needed something to blame all my troubles on, and I often blamed southern Ohio. If I could just get away from here, I thought, everything would be better.

Though things often don't turn out the way you think they will, I now like to believe they usually turn out the way they're supposed to if you hang in there long enough. In my case, I ended up in an alcohol and drug rehab in Portsmouth, down by the Ohio River. After my head cleared up a little, I started to see that all my problems were of my own making, that blaming the place where I was born or other people for my troubles was ridiculous, to say the least. I stayed sober and slowly began to carve out a new life for myself; and a few years later, I decided to try to learn how to write. For a long time, I filled my stories with doctors and lawyers and professors, people I knew nothing about, in places like Boston and Los Angeles, mainly because I didn't think anyone would be interested in reading about the rural Midwest and its inhabitants. Everything I wrote fell flat and lifeless on the page until I finally began to set my fiction in southern Ohio. As I kept writing about it, I began to see the place in a new light, which is, I think, one of the chief things that art is supposed to do. True, there is a lot of ugliness and despair and heartbreak in these hills, but there is also much goodness and mystery and beauty. The stunning poetry and prose chosen by Neil Carpathios for this anthology is ample proof of that.

Now that I've published a couple of books, people ask me from time to time if I'll ever leave southern Ohio. I suppose many of them figure, as I once did, that a writer would be better off in a big city or a picturesque village in New England or a secluded cabin in the Rockies. But I mean it with all my heart when I say, "No, I can't think of anywhere I'd rather live." Some of them understand and some don't; and, of course, a few years ago that answer would have certainly surprised me. Not anymore though. Last week I was at a gas station near my house buying a cup of coffee when I heard a store clerk practically begging a customer, an old, befuddled-looking man wearing dirty tennis shoes and clutching a ten-dollar bill, not to spend any more money on lottery tickets. There's a story there, and I hope to hell I can write it someday.

—Donald Ray Pollock

INTRODUCTION

The singer and songwriter Tom Waits says in one of his songs: "I never saw my hometown until I stayed away too long." So much about a place—its essence and personal impact—is a matter of perspective. Maybe only after a period of absence can one return to see a landscape and people with true clarity. But what about the experience of someone who moves to a new place and for the first time witnesses its unique qualities, its beauties, its scars, its quirky and fascinating traits? Doesn't this newcomer, at the very least, crave some understanding of his new home?

Six years ago I moved to southern Ohio to teach creative writing at Shawnee State University in Portsmouth. I had never been south of Columbus. As hard as that might be to believe, it is true. I had driven through southern Ohio to get somewhere else, but never stayed in the region for more than a few hours. I have lived most of my life in northeastern Ohio in the Akron-Canton area. It did not take long for southern Ohio's rolling hills, Ohio River, Appalachian culture, southern twang dialect, warm weather, copious deer, outdoor markets, down-home friendliness, and sturdy moral backbone—as well as a lacerating economic and substance-abuse scenario—to begin imprinting me with a profound sense of place. Sure, northern Ohio has its own special features as part of the Rust Belt, but I felt and still feel that southern Ohio swirls with a more primal, haunting beauty that I struggle to define. I cannot claim, as a newer southern Ohio resident, to offer original insights, and I would never presume to insult those who have long lived here and understand better than anyone the hidden bones of this land through generations. Yet I have felt a desire to better appreciate this region, and its place in the overall scheme of Appalachia. Which brings up Appalachia itself.

I've heard it said that you can't understand America until you understand Appalachia. Any textbook will provide a place to start—the surface facts.

The region, as defined by the Appalachian Regional Commission (ARC), which was established in 1965 by President Lyndon B. Johnson, is a 205,000-square-mile area that follows the spine of the Appalachian Mountains from southern New York to northern Mississippi. It includes all of West Virginia and parts of twelve other states: Alabama, Georgia, Kentucky, Maryland, Mississippi, New York, North Carolina, Ohio, Pennsylvania, South Carolina, Tennessee, and Virginia. Various Native American hunter-gatherer tribes covered the area 16,000 years ago. The majority of the region now comprises mostly Anglo-Scottish descendants, along with many Irish and German who migrated from Europe in the eighteenth century. Twenty-five million people (42 percent of Appalachians) live in rural areas, in contrast with 20 percent of the national population. This, of course, is critical to Appalachia's history. The region's economy mainly distinguished itself through mining, forestry, and agriculture, but obsolete farming methods and unemployment due to mechanized mining techniques left much of Appalachia impoverished. In the 1950s and 1960s many unemployed residents of Appalachia migrated to places like Akron and Cleveland and other urban locales in search of jobs. So, although Appalachia is recognized as a distinctive region, its citizens have branched out, extending bloodlines to other areas. When I lived in northeastern Ohio, many of my neighbors had grandparents and great-grandparents living in rural southern Ohio, West Virginia, Kentucky, and other areas of Appalachia.

Like many people outside Appalachia, I was familiar with some of the common stereotypes of Appalachians perpetuated in the media. I pictured Jed Clampett from the television show *The Beverly Hillbillies*, or a Daniel Boone–type character wearing a coonskin cap and buckskin clothing and toting a long rifle. I had heard of the infamous feuding Kentucky and West Virginia clans known as the Hatfields and the McCoys and envisioned Appalachians as tough customers not to be messed with. The James Dickey novel *Deliverance* and the movie of the same name tickled my overactive imagination into conjuring a bunch of baccer-spittin', barefooted mountain folk hovering around a homemade metal vat under the cover of night, creating the untaxed backwoods brew known as "moonshine," secretly stirring by the light of the moon. I imagined snake-handling ceremonies, people speaking in tongues, faith healing, and natural cures. I pictured hardship-toughened geezers rocking on dilapidated porches, spitting and cursing at the way the world keeps changing. I knew that, surely, these were inaccurate exaggerations, but the power of the imagery's effect on the psyche could not be denied.

I also had heard some of the Appalachian lore, so often displaying the Appalachian connection to the land: Plowing on Good Friday will cause the ground to bleed. The number of seeds in an apple will be your lucky number. Redheaded gardeners grow hotter peppers. Eating sugar before planting fruit trees makes for sweeter fruit. Of course, like most lore, such beliefs vary by region and are often long removed from contemporary life. But again, a cumulative and deficient sense of what an Appalachian was may have been taking root.

Many Appalachian pioneers who moved into areas isolated by mountain ridges had to fend for themselves in grueling conditions, and this in some ways may have contributed to their self-sufficient ruggedness and often fierce sense of independence; nonetheless, media-driven misrepresentations distort the truth and cheat many Appalachians of their true essence. Yes, Appalachia is greatly rural. Yes, more people in the region hunt and fish and live off the land than in many other places. Yes, there is poverty. But it is a lazy and unfair oversimplification to encapsulate a whole domain and its citizens in such narrow terms.

Appalachian life thrums with paradox. This is apparent on a daily basis. Some residents of the area adapt to and even embrace the isolation that results from geography and economic limitations, while others despise it. Strong family ties and loyalty to a sense of place persist alongside a growing youth population's dreams of escape. A resistance to change and a desire to retain traditional Appalachian ways are offset by accelerated modernization and outmigration by a younger generation hungry for the new. In my handful of years as an educator in Appalachian Ohio, I have worked with many individuals who were first-generation college students. The families of these young people, according to the students themselves, have been proud yet sometimes resentful. Parents often feel acceptance and admiration but also abandonment. The land is no different, chock-full of a tension of opposites. The beauty of lush hills and forests is checked by the ugliness of buildings and homes allowed to crumble due to poverty; and the indigenous wealth of coal is countered by the exploitation of human and natural resources exercised by a volatile coal economy. I've seen people living in cardboard boxes down by the river as well as a local university and hospital blossoming, gaining recognition on a national level for excellence. More often than in any other place I've lived, I have stood in checkout lines fumbling with coins, coming up a penny or two short, and had the person behind me step forward to give the cashier the needed change. More often than in any other place, I have seen despondent men and women in electric wheelchairs on sidewalks and in parks drinking out of paper sacks. It is this very contradiction that intrigues and haunts.

With the creation of the Appalachian Regional Commission, there have been significant improvements in transportation, education, health care, and other social infrastructure. Despite the continuing challenge of improving a region whose size and diversity complicate easy solutions, the number of economically distressed Appalachian counties decreased from 223 in 1965 to 98 in 2013. Behind these changes is the evidence of a more genuine commitment to the region's reality, as opposed to its mythology, by politicians and funding organizations. This has led to improved awareness as well as tangible results. Such a naturally beautiful land, full of spirited, vibrant, and proud citizens, deserves this and more.

Appalachian Ohio is considered part of Central Appalachia (southeastern Ohio, eastern Kentucky, and most of West Virginia) and is marked by its location at the foothills of the Appalachian Mountains. The Ohio River also is a powerful and distinguishing feature, like a long liquid muscle constantly flexing—muddy, majestic. The landscape, the warmer weather, and the slower pace of life give this part of the state a southern flavor. Thirty-two of Ohio's eighty-eight counties make up the region, which contains one-third of the state's land and 12.9 percent of all Ohioans. No county has more than 63,000 people, which encourages a strong sense of community. In general, the people share many of the cultural traits of greater Appalachia, with prominent northwestern European roots, unlike northern Ohio's and the Rust Belt's more ethnically and racially diverse population. This relative homogeneity contributes to a certain tight-knittedness and aura of pride. Farmers markets, quilting and crafts, and Appalachian folk music are ever-present as well.

However, the region is more than just hills and hollows. World-class manufacturing exists in the form of chemical, plastic, metal, automotive, ceramic, and wood products. Power plants benefit from cheap water transport, and although most of the region's mines have closed, Monroe County remains one of the most productive mining territories in the nation. Education is another strong point. Higher education thrives with Ohio

University in Athens and its five branch campuses. This is a major training and education resource, complemented by other fine public institutions such as Miami University in Oxford, Rio Grande University, and Ohio's newest public university, established in 1986, Shawnee State. Various private colleges also exist, and no county is more than an hour's drive from a vocational education source.

As with all places, new challenges continue to present themselves. One of these has been the recent drug problem. In southeastern Ohio, marijuana and meth production stubbornly persist, and in Scioto County, my new home, a painkiller called OxyContin and its distribution by a handful of licensed doctors running "pill mills" have drawn national attention. Although other areas of Appalachia and the nation in general have similar problems, Ohio's southernmost counties have been identified, sadly, as ground zero. Portsmouth sits at the juncture of three states—Ohio, Kentucky, and West Virginia—and has a major north-south artery, U.S. 23, that runs through on its path from Michigan to Florida. The overlapping of jurisdictions, the freeway pipeline, and continued struggles with poverty create a perfect storm for the drug trade. But even the effort to combat illegal drugs has made gains in recent years. Crooked doctors have been arrested. Pill mills have been shut down. The fight continues.

Despite economic struggles typical of other Appalachian areas, especially those with a scarred mining past, the region boasts some of America's most breathtaking land, from the Hocking Hills in Hocking County to Ross County's tree-lined cliffs, to the Shawnee State Forest in Scioto County and Vesuvius Lake in Lawrence County. Ecotourism continues to provide a welcome influx of commerce. State parks and forests offer some of the nation's finest campgrounds, hiking trails, and fishing spots. But more than this, there seems to be an almost dreamy sense of time. I have watched the morning haze slowly rise into the hills and the Ohio River lapping, luring me out of my selfish concerns toward something beyond the physical. I consider myself lucky to be able to step outside on any given day to explore, experience, and learn. I happily admit to being smitten by the trees, hills, rivers, and streams that flourish beyond the scope of statistics or data.

Indeed, surface facts can supply only so much information. Appalachian Ohio's essence, its sometimes mysterious and paradoxical nature, cannot be so easily or neatly packaged, labeled, and shelved. In the spirit of further exploration, I have turned to the poetry and stories I not only love but believe can convey truth more deeply and humanly than other pedagogical modes of transmission. I, myself, am a poet, and it is fellow poets and creative writers that I have long relied upon to get closer to the heart of a subject.

So, in truth, this anthology started with a personal, maybe even somewhat selfish desire, to better grasp my new home. I sent out a call for submissions locally and nationally through various media. I asked for poetry, fiction, and nonfiction that in some way reflected, or connected to, Appalachian Ohio life. I received more than four hundred submissions from writers who have at some point lived here or still live here. It quickly became clear that there are many passionate and gifted people who have been influenced by the bottom half of our state. Many of the writers are accomplished authors, and many are less known. Regardless, they continue the tradition of Appalachian writing that connects all Appalachians to each other and has long been cherished by the whole nation—writers such as James Agee, James Still, Jesse Stuart, Wendell Berry, Jo Carson, Ron Rash, Dorothy Allison, Rachel Carson, Jim Wayne Miller, Gurney Norman, and the recent Affrilachian poets led by Frank X. Walker and Nikky Finney—just to name a few. I am grateful for all who provided their works, their encouragement, their willing participation. Because of them, this book is a reality.

Aside from a personal desire to gather a group of voices, I also envisioned a book to provide valuable information for others, not only in Appalachia but beyond. What better way to know a place than through personal and artistic outpourings marked by a concrete sensory specificity that is the lifeblood of creative writing? No historical text, despite its facts, can capture the subtle nuances and shades of color that exist in the palpable realm we call real life. A book like this is magical, in this sense. It bears a collective psychic fingerprint of Appalachia—in this case, the Ohio "finger" of Appalachia's "hand." It is my hope that in the pages to follow the reader will not merely get an aerial view of Appalachian Ohio's legacy and landscape—which is more what a history book offers—but also an intense close-up of the people, their hopes and dreams and impressions. As you read, feel the rich dark soil underfoot, smell a pie baking in the other room, hear the Ohio River rolling and the voice of a farmer's wife calling to her children.

In making selections for this collection, my primary criterion was quality. I also wanted to include a variety of styles, subjects, and voices. Beyond this, I did not have any preconceived vision of what I would end up with or how I would arrange the book. Only after I had chosen individual pieces did I step back and try to identify overarching themes. This anthology seemed to take on a life of its own, organically falling into four sections. In hindsight, the sections do logically cover what one might envision for life in Appalachian Ohio, touching on many of the characteristic traits of the region already mentioned in this introduction (family, people, nature, hardship, a sense of home as well as displacement). Many of the works within a particular section include elements typical of other sections. For instance, a poem or story in the "Family and Folks" section may include nature references that could suggest placement with other nature-oriented pieces in "The Land." Similarly, a piece in the section titled "The Grind" might include family situations that could possibly point to the "Family and Folks" section. In the section that I call "Home and Away," there are many pieces that feature themes concerning people, nature, and elements of daily living. The reader will notice, then, an interweaving and overlapping, and I am pleased by this result, as it more realistically captures true life, time, and memory, which can be complex. The real world is not broken into categories and labeled for us. However, the sections at least allow for a certain order and framework, and a place for the reader to start exploring.

In addition, I had to loosely define what I considered Appalachian Ohio. While nearly all of the pieces reflect the state below Columbus, which is often viewed as the center boundary line of Ohio, there is mention, here and there, of a landmark or experience that in part references something a bit north of that line.

THE FIRST SECTION, "Family and Folks," includes works that are most strongly marked by a sense of character. A significant trait of Appalachian life is the connection to family and community. The people in these pieces display the uniqueness of personality typical of the region's family and folks. Roy Bentley, David Lee Garrison, and Beverly Zeimer lovingly recall their grandmothers, the maternal figureheads that loom so large in Appalachian family structures. In "Stubborn Roots," Preston Martin shares how an exotic plant comes to embody a grandfather's deeply rooted love. In his novel chapter, "The Offer," Ed Davis takes us inside the home of his character, Cloyd, whose family is dealing with a sense of loss, as a special visitor helps highlight many of the tastes and traditions of Appalachian hospitality and ignites unexpected passions. Idiosyncratic neighbors appear, such as Bertha, who welcomes poet Jeanne Bryner to the neighborhood, and Stevie, who actually lives in a silo in David Baker's poem "Outside." The section closes with two poems, by Diane Kendig and Michael Waterson, that reference perhaps Appalachian Ohio's favorite poetic son: James Wright. Wright captured so much about this part of our state, and the writers here pay homage.

The second section, "The Land," contains writings that reveal aspects of the landscape and wildlife, so much a part of this rural terrain. From hills to creeks, from sycamores to cardinals, from horses to even a theater of cows—the pieces here remind us that when vividly rendered, the natural world can almost be tasted through the senses. Indeed, in Christopher Citro's poem "Wine Tasting, Nine A.M.," the speaker samples "traces of thin clouds filtering / the universe as it comes to us in this town, / leaving discernible flavors." In "Beside Spring Creek," Cathryn Essinger describes the mysterious sense of presence that can occur in nature, when she sees "in the watery shadows, the hand on my shoulder, / warm and familiar, that causes me to look up, / even when there is no one there." Richard Hague's fine essay "Sycamore Country" is a sort of love song to one of the region's most identifiable and beautiful trees, and despite his more urban trappings, he realizes that some things like trees and birds provide "news more important than is covered on most of TV." Julie L. Moore even humorously relates how a poet, often rejected by editors, can find a kinder and more appreciative audience in an open-air theater of cows that "watch you like spectators, like fans."

The third section, titled "The Grind," recognizes some of the hardships inherent to life for certain individuals in Appalachian Ohio. A struggle—to survive, to thrive, to find peace in the face of economic, familial, and national stress—surfaces through characters and voices grinding to overcome circumstances. The speaker in Laura Madeline Wiseman's poem "In Line for the Cashier" can't help noticing a man with a shopping cart full of cat food cans, which leads her to wonder about the man's hunger as she sees his "threadbare corduroys, the knobby wrists / jutting from the second-hand sweater." In his powerful short fiction "Coming Home," Michael Henson tells the story of opiate-addicted Maggie Boylan, who returns home after being released from a treatment facility for drug rehab and encounters old and new demons to joust with. In her short story "The

Last Shot," Christina Jones paints a portrait of how job loss can lead one to desperate acts: a life of crime, or even worse. In "Destroying New Boston," Brooks Rexroat's fictional characters reveal how people in a town whose industry has decayed might act in surprising and destructive ways. Donald Ray Pollock's story "The Jesus Lights" vibrates with loss and suffering, as a man and his wife grapple with the weight of each other's pain against the backdrop of a town called Knockemstiff. And yet, in his poem "Psalm 96," Joel Peckham reminds us of that certain Appalachian perseverance against the odds that one sees, and how there can be a sort of singing "to the Lord because the Lord is hope that maybe a new song / can rise."

The last and largest section, "Home and Away," is characterized by a deep sense of place. Contributors address what it is like to live in Appalachian Ohio, to move away and look back, and to pass through. In Cathy Cultice Lentes's poem, the speaker sympathizes with a young man who misses the hills of Appalachia. Similarly, in the short story "The Stars in Shawnee," Dallas Woodburn's character Eleanor, who lives in Los Angeles, cannot forget the sunsets and sky of her childhood Ohio home. Nostalgic childhood memories of 1950s southern Ohio are shared by Ronald D. Giles in his nonfiction piece "The Friday Night Dance." Myrna Stone follows with poems about childhood experiences in southern Ohio in "The Girls Play Dress-Up" and "Pyrotechnicalities." In her nonfiction "Painting Portsmouth," Tanya Bomsta provides a portrait of Portsmouth, Ohio, some of its history and landmarks. One can even sense an undercurrent of mountain music and an emotional directness typical of Appalachia's rich oral tradition of ballads and folk songs in Jennifer Schomburg Kanke's "caution: do not use with mono devices" and Rebecca J. R. Lachman's "Tourist Brochure of Athens, Ohio"—both poems anthems of pride about Appalachian Ohio.

I asked each contributor to include a brief statement to introduce his or her work, and its Appalachian Ohio connection. I felt this would serve almost as a frame to the writer's "pictures" or "portraits" on display. These conversational entryways convey a personal touch, a warm feel, as if the writer is saying hello, shaking your hand, opening up to you. The contributors' statements are located with the authors' biographical sketches at book's end.

I WANT TO recognize several people, without whom this project would not have been possible. First, I am grateful to Gillian Berchowitz, Director of Ohio University Press. She was receptive and excited about this project when I approached her, and her encouragement and expertise were my guiding light. A big thank you goes to my home university, Shawnee State. My colleagues have been, as ever, supportive beyond measure. In addition, I was fortunate to be given financial assistance to help fund certain aspects of the process through a university grant. Eric Braun, Director of Development, and the university as a whole recognized the value of this anthology. Thank you to my two amazing, hard-working editorial assistants: Kelly Grooms and Matt McGuire. They put in long hours at various stages, and their camaraderie and keen insights were invaluable. And finally, of course, I must thank my wife, Carole. Not only was she always patient and encouraging, but she helped immensely with the technology of formatting the manuscript prior to final production.

The title of this anthology comes from the poem of the same name by David Lee Garrison. The speaker in that poem describes what at first seems a typical midwestern experience: looking at snow. But then something happens. He is bonded with a sort of universal, planetary essence, and he states that suddenly he sees "every river on earth." A moment in time in a certain place can be at the same time simple and natural as well as complex and mysterious. It can provide a gateway to a larger world. Maybe we can better understand Appalachia as a whole by sampling the voices gathered here. Maybe we can better comprehend our interconnectedness as a nation, whatever patch of earth we occupy. I hope that this anthology, or certain individual works within, might allow you, the reader, to experience this part of Appalachia and even reach through and past it to a wider, more profound sense of wonder.

ONE

FAMILY AND FOLKS

Mirror, Brush & Comb

In a rectangle of window light that falls on her bed
my grandmother sits unwrapping Christmas gifts.

This is a day of ribbons and patterned paper
dropped like currency at the feet of a woman.
The next opened box holds the gilded tools
of looking presentable. She hands it back,
saying, *Oh, honey, this is too nice for me.*
I'm a kid; I know to say nothing and watch.

My mother takes the box, stepping into the sun's
idea of the true and beautiful in Ohio in December.
Whatever light doesn't fall on her divvies itself
into a fractious Braille on the chenille bedspread.
I watch my mother place the present on the bed.
And I see it takes patience to live in this world.

How long will this gift-giving go on? Longer
than a boy of five accepts without fidgeting.

Still, you ought to have seen what I saw—
a woman rumored to have shot at a man,
working her tongue against a last remaining tooth:
a figure spent from storybook disappointments:
a stranger with white hair and a look on her face
I can only describe as fierce, reaching at last

for what's been mislaid. As if it were love,
precious in the stiff fingers of either hand.

ROY BENTLEY

Far

Tonight, I'm reading to my grandmother Potter who
only attended school as far as the 3rd grade. I read her
the opening pyrotechnics of The Book of Revelation,
and I know that Granny really wants me to read myself
to sleep, but I'm not that sleepy. I read on. There's some
Old Testament story of King David that I've flipped to
that mentions foreskins and Philistines. Farther on, these
same Philistines are having to hand over their foreskins,
so of course I ask what all that means. She tells me that
I'm circumcised but how it just means cut down there.
She lowers her bi-focals. And points and says the word
tallywacker and we laugh. She likes for me to read aloud
but doesn't like me to ask her what words mean because
it causes her to have to say That's far enough for tonight
and then revisit the sad fact she doesn't know that much
about language beyond how far to take it, which is pretty
far since she is building a life on the words. She won't
cut her hair or drink liquor or say Those Words, words
you know without me saying, because she is far enough
along in her revelation to think she shouldn't. Which is
sort of odd to my mind. I like beer and she tells the story
of having to church-key open a can of Budweiser for me.
At 2, I had my very own can of beer. Anyway, I put my
heart and soul into reading. I travel to far-off Jerusalem.
I hear about the Crucifixion and the Resurrection. I think
The Gospel According to Mazy Frances Collier Potter,
but what I know is that my parents are divorced and
in 1962 not one of the families on our street will let
their kids to play with me. I'm pretty sure the ones
Jesus came to save aren't worth saving. Far from it.
Any kid who reads aloud from the King James Bible

4   EVERY RIVER ON EARTH

thinks he's as smart as Bugs Bunny or the Road Runner.
Thinks he knows something only he knows. Like: that
adults are a danger to themselves and others, and prone
to turning all creation upside down like a piggybank.
Then she tells me you can't make someone love you.
Which is damn smart for anyone who didn't make it
far beyond the 3rd grade and who keeps her false teeth
in a glass by her bedside and keeps knocking the glass
over but can't finally figure how far is too far to reach.

ROY BENTLEY

A Night in 1962

There used to be a way my uncle put his feet up,
my Abe Lincoln–thin uncle from the Kentucky hills,
shoes off and crossing his ankles on a coffee table,
that said the day's work was over. Most nights,
he came home wearing work pants and a shirt
with an oval patch above the pocket. The patch
said Bill. I knew that if I looked there would be
grease under his fingernails. Whatever he did,
the doing of it seemed to have entered his body.
I'd watch him light a cigarette, inhale and let the
smoke fill the den like the burn was a refutation
of men he worked with who mocked his accent,
the cloud itself a kind of totem against the factory.
And he'd check his Bulova wristwatch—the hour
after midnight and me awake, my boy-presence
something he never minded. If his feet stank,
he knew it; and though it was an earned odor,
it was one for which he'd often apologize as
white-gray clouds took their motions from his,
cartwheeling in a bluish tide of TV-screen light.
Most nights, a black-and-white western with
the sound off so as not to wake Aunt Helen
who'd likely rouse regardless and waltz in,
asking how his shift at Frigidaire had gone.
If he drank a beer, it was from the can. Two
triangular slits, one on either side of the can,
and a frothy foam escaping after each swig.
A beer and a filterless Camel his reward—
and a place to put his feet up without fear
of criticism, a man filled with kind words
for anyone who would sit for an hour and
hear spoken the brave language of Work.

Folding Tables and Five-Card Stud

Gospel hour on the radio
and my grandmother joined in
Yes, we'll gather at the river,
the beautiful, the beautiful river . . .
Then she told me about Sunday mornings
when the congregation was haunted
by that cry from the pulpit,
"Where will *you* spend eternity?"
About camp meetings
where they barked Satan up a tree,
and people who got saved or healed
would tremble for days on end;
about river baptisms
with the preacher holding one arm
and a deacon the other
because the current was so swift
that converts had been known
to slip from reach and drown.

She joked that Baptists
never make love standing up
because it's too much like dancing,
and she confided that Brother Felthouse
always called a *card table*
a *folding table*
because he didn't want his flock
getting any ideas.

Sometimes, before Granny dealt
the first hand of the evening,
she would ask the whole family to

Please rise and sing
our invitation hymn,
"Just As I Am."
After the first few lines,
the only ones we knew,
she would say, "Amen, brothers and sisters!
Now ante up, the game is five-card stud!"

Peace in a Primitive Place

for Grandma

I looked for you down Old Xenia Road,
and near the heart of Paint Creek Fork,
past the caretaker's house,
stark white against a cerulean sky,
a green-painted pony-truss bridge.

I found you in a hill of sedge,
facing off, with a Shawnee Indian chief,
the southern native wood
of burr oaks, hickories, sugar maples
and white marble stones.

All around, signs of life—
bright green field corn, lively cardinals
in the flowering shrubs.
Your simple love of life in this place.
Your tobacco pipe at the bottom of the run.

Ohio Lightning

My bed was near a window
where the storms
came in on summer nights but when
the thunder rolled and lightning cracked the sky,
my warring parents put down their bitter weapons
and rushed into my room as the rain poured in
and the curtains blew, afraid I might get struck
by lightning as I slept, my father in his
striped pajamas, mother in a silken gown
long red hair around her. This image lodges still.
Now that they are gone I dream of them and
everything has changed. They sit at a table
in their bedroom eating breakfast looking
at each other. Their eyes are sparkling.
The room is painted white.

Stubborn Roots

When his young wife died during childbirth
he became a full-time father.
Neighbors stepped up and watched the child
in the early years so he could work the fields.
"But I'm the one who will raise her," Benny said.
And he did.

By the time I knew him he leaned on a cane
and spent afternoons on the porch watching clouds.
He lifted me to his lap and told me stories.
I took hold of his hand when we walked in the yard,
his skin as cool and smooth as leather.
When he broke his hip he was sorry
to be a burden. In the rest home he acted
content to the end.

As a young man in the thirties, after setting tobacco,
he walked into town. In the store his eye caught
an exotic plant potted in a coffee can.
The plant came with a warning that he laughed off.
He brought it home for his little girl
and set it in the bald hill behind the house.
Eighty years on his daughter
is resigned the bamboo will outlive her,
her children, and the land itself.
It withstands the winters and when a plant dies
on its own, two shoots peek out of the ground.
And every night, unless there are clouds,
the setting sun backlights the willowy culms
and exotic leaves
that wave on the hillside all the way to the creek.

Enough to Go Around

RR 1 West Jefferson, Ohio, 1950—for Daddy

Next to nothing was in the root cellar—
a few potatoes and onions—
the slab of jowl to season the beans
strung from the rafters,
a five-gallon bucket of lard.

The Old Farmer's Almanac,
covenant between you and the earth,
hung on its nail,
the moon and gales
all in their proper places.

You dug us out of a snowstorm
the next day.

Stomping on the back porch,
you swept snow from your overalls
with Grandma's broom,
carried in a gray and white rabbit
by its hind legs.

You brought the cold inside
and warmed us,
laid the rabbit out on the worn linoleum floor,
we gathered around to pet it,
and see the buckshot.

Mommy said,
"There won't be enough to go around."

You ripped the fur down over its skinny belly,
filled the cottage
with the sweet smell of meat
floured and fried brown in spattering grease.
At suppertime, we all got a taste.

Beverly Zeimer

The Offer

Maggie didn't know what she was expecting but upon entering the house, her first observation was how clean it was. It was dark in the kitchen with only one window—in fact, it was dark everywhere in this old, old house more than a hundred years old (the oldest, Dad had told her, the first one built on the ridge in 1872). Had she expected the hill man's house to be dirty, cluttered, a widower's nightmare?

A tall woman wearing a blue bandana on her head stood at the sink shucking corn, her shoulders bent. A young girl, six or seven and wearing a plain blue dress, knelt on a kitchen chair, patting down modeling clay on the table—not that smelly Play-Doh but real clay. She couldn't recall the last time she'd seen the stuff, so hard and inflexible until, after rolling it between your palms for many minutes, it warmed to your body's temperature and became moldable.

"This is Margaret Absher." Cloyd's voice seemed too loud in the high-ceilinged kitchen. Maggie watched the shoulders of the corn-shucker tense. For a moment, the only sound was the boiling water on the stove, a Hotpoint like her grandmother's, back in Kentucky. When the woman at the sink didn't turn around, Maggie looked at the child. Golden was the only word for her, her blonde hair a ball of crackling energy in the sunset glow from the window behind her.

"Margaret is George Wright's daughter."

The child's dark eyes widened before she thunked down the clay from her fingers on the table. Then she leapt down from her the chair and ran to the newcomer, hugging her thighs, laying her cheek against Maggie's stomach. Nearly reeling, Maggie let out a sound of startle before laughing. Glancing up, she gazed directly into the eyes of the scowling woman now half-turned from her task at the sink. She looked about thirty, her dark eyes fierce.

"Lily Clair!" Turning from the sink, the woman swabbed her hands on her frilly apron, stepped over and attempted to peel the girl's hands off Maggie's thighs.

"It's all right," Maggie said. "She's just—"

"Let go, child. NOW." She bent over, tearing at the girl's fingers. Still the woman wouldn't look at Maggie, who was surprised to find herself relaxed—and curious. Was the young woman a sister, housekeeper, baby-sitter—all three? She wore stylishly torn jeans, dangling hoop earrings and fire-engine-red lipstick, and was very, very thin, her long arms bony.

"Let go of her!"

Maggie patted the girl's back, surrendering the way she would to an over-friendly dog. The girl clung fiercely, shaking her curls. "Uncle George!" she shouted, though her voice was muffled against Maggie's blouse.

"Hush, now. That's not George. It's only his daughter."

No louder than before but firm as granite, Cloyd's voice cut through the tangle created by the three female bodies: "Lily Clair. Let go of Margaret, please." Instantly the child released Maggie and stepped back, staring up at her as if she were God's wife, making Maggie blush in spite of herself.

"Uncle George," the girl whispered.

"Yes, sweetheart, he's my father," Maggie said. "My name is—"

"Margaret, let us all set down." Maggie felt the tiniest wave of resistance flick through her, as she turned toward Cloyd's voice, recalling her father saying men ruled the roost in Marshall County, chuckling as he added, "But the women rule the nest!"

"Percy, bring the food, and I'll say grace. Unless you'd like to, Margaret."

Maggie shook her head and lowered her eyes, feeling perhaps as intimidated as Cloyd might've felt in her father's presence. The golden child got back up on her chair, sitting correctly, hands folded in her lap. Cloyd picked up the clay and placed it on the sideboard behind her. When Lily bowed her head, Maggie quickly sat, her eyes shut tight.

"Dear heavenly father, bless this food to the nourishment of our body and soul. And thank you for this visitor, who traveled far and shared so generously this day. Also—"

During the pause, Maggie heard the swishing of Lily's legs as they fanned the still air and felt, as if fingers on the back of her neck, the corn-shucker's eyes on her, causing her face to warm again. Who was the woman and why was she so hostile? Was it the destruction Maggie had wrought making her unwelcome here? "It takes time to be accepted down there," George had said more than once.

"—accept your bounty and the gift of eternal life with all the gratitude in our heart, Lord. And—"

It seemed incredible to Maggie that a man with Cloyd's great loss felt so grateful. For now, that fact obscured any resentment coming from the cook (and nanny?) standing behind her. As long as he wanted her here—the man who, she realized, now stood for all those she had wronged here with her great sin—maybe she could bear this woman's enmity.

"Amen," she said aloud. She opened her eyes to see Cloyd in the shadows at the opposite end of the table, hands still tented. Behind her, the woman exploded into high-pitched laughter.

"Good job, Margaret. If you hadn't of amen-ed him, he might've prayed till the milk clabbered and the cock crowed." A bejeweled hand plunked down a platter of steaming corn ("roastin ears," her Grandma called them) in front of her. "I'm Percy, by the way." Plopping into the chair on Maggie's right, she grinned. Maggie gazed, open-mouthed. With her kerchief removed, shoulder-length red hair the color of polished cherry spilled down the sides of her face. While her long face was not conventionally beautiful, Maggie thought it was the most interesting face she'd ever seen, though, if asked why, she could not have answered.

Ignoring her, Cloyd unclasped his hands and reached for the biscuits, and for the next three minutes, Maggie joined the ritual she hadn't realized she'd lost when those Sunday dinners at Grandma's had ceased after The Big Fallout with the Kentucky relatives. In and out of hands passed gleaming red and yellow tomatoes bigger than softballs, golden-fried chicken, fat biscuits, white milk gravy and green beans salty with fat pork, onions and black pepper. Among the dishes were a jar of chou-chou Cloyd heaped on his beans, and mashed potatoes whipped to cloud-fluff. Cloyd, she saw, dipped his cucumbers into a salt-filled saucer just like her grand-daddy had. Tempted to carve the chicken breast on her plate with knife and fork, instead Maggie, following Cloyd's example, picked it up with her fingers and bit into the crisp skin. It tasted nothing like the chaste, dry baked chicken she made, mostly to cut fat and calories. All was silent except the sounds of chewing for a few minutes. Looking to her right, she noticed Percy staring at her.

Maggie laid the chicken on her plate. "What?"

"You act like you ain't ever bit into a fryer before, Margaret."

Maggie laughed and picked up the breast again. "My grandmother used to make hers just like this, on"—she turned to point—"a stove exactly like that one."

"That right?" She leaned on her elbows. "Where was your granny from?"

"Logan, Kentucky. We went every Christmas and summer to see her."

"You's raised somewhere else, though."

"Dayton. Mom met Dad in college at UD—University of Dayton—and never went back."

"*Never went back home?*" When the woman squinted at her, Maggie knew she'd told too much. The Kentucky kin finally just couldn't handle her mother marrying a Catholic and getting above her raisin's. So they'd disowned her—but not before she had disowned them.

"No. I haven't seen any of my cousins in thirty years."

"Mercy sakes! How 'bout your greats?" Leaning forward, Percy stared in disbelief, the hoops in her ears swaying.

Maggie shook her head and lowered her eyes, embarrassed at something that hadn't mattered to anyone else in her acquaintance—until this minute. She'd lost interest in eating any more of the chicken that lay neglected on her plate. Glancing across the table, she saw the child swirling her fork around in her mashed potatoes. It didn't look as though she'd eaten a bite.

"Well, I swan." Percy reared back in her chair as if now she'd heard everything. "Did you hear that, Cloyd? No kinfolk whatever."

If he heard, it didn't disturb him enough to interfere with his sopping up dollops of gravy with his biscuit. He never looked up. Irritated by how red her cheeks must be shining, Maggie didn't look away, obligated to stand her ground in the face of this woman's shaming attitude.

Unfolding her arms, Percy stared, her eyes glowing with liquid fire. Just when Maggie was certain she'd start tsk-tsking, the woman bent forward, stretched out a long arm and grazed her cheek with long, tallow fingers.

"I'm so sorry," she whispered. "That is so sad."

Maggie could not have been more mesmerized by a hooded cobra. As she watched in fascination, the woman leaned back and refolded her arms, wearing an inscrutable smile that could've been either sisterly or a smirk.

Before she could think of something to say, Cloyd looked up and pointed.

"Eat, Percy."

She sprang up as if he'd jabbed her with a knife. "No, I'll eat a bite with Cale. He said he'd be late this evening, not to hold supper, so I'll just wrap him up some o' this—"

"No." Head down, Cloyd sucked on his corncob—had he done that in front of his wife? Maggie wondered.

"Why the hell not?" Hands on the table, Percy leaned aggressively toward him. Maggie watched the child look from one to the other, interested but apparently not fearful. Percy stepped back, keeping her gaze riveted on the man she'd cooked for—sister, Maggie was now certain, though they didn't look anything alike. *Maybe stepsister?*

"He's always late, if he bothers to come home at all. And if he's drunk—"

"So what?" She threw up her arms, then flung herself forward to lean on the table, bending so far forward, Maggie could see the tops of her breasts, ill-contained in a skimpy halter beneath the apron. "Cale works hard as you!" She shouted. "He buys groceries. He pays half the bills."

She stood back up. Though the little girl's eyes were wide, she didn't look panicked. She'd seen and heard it all before.

"He's young, that's all. Do you remember, Cloyd Cluny, what it means to be young?"

He looked up sharply, blue eyes afire. "I know what it means to surrender to the wiles of the Evil One. I know what it means to dangle over the pit holding onto a thin branch while the flames lick your feet."

Evil One. It took Maggie back to Grandma's church, so different from Holy Blood, near UD's campus, where Maggie had attended every Sunday mass until she'd married Mark. At Grandma's church, a succession of preachers—not one of them seminary-trained—stood and shouted sermons while members of the congregation fired his words back to him in loud, staccatto bursts. Now here was this gentle man, Maggie's defender, sounding for all the world like a Primitive Baptist!

"Yeah, I guess you do know what it is to hang above the pit." She turned to Maggie and smiled. "Once upon a time, Cloyd was known to take a wee snort of old John Barleycorn."

Maggie absorbed the information with as blank a look as she could muster, though her heart had begun beating faster. *Who was this woman and why was she being so nasty?*

Turning her attention back to Cloyd, Percy leaned on her elbows. "But you didn't fall. What makes you think your brother will?"

Now Cloyd was licking his fingers. Calmly, without looking up, he said. "You, Percy. He could spend eternity in hell because of you."

The only visible reaction was Lily's. She looked at her plate, which was still untouched. Maybe this was new. Maggie found anger now warring with sadness, as she wanted to tell them both to shut up, for Lily's sake. Maggie decided she could at least excuse herself from such a display. Words of parting were on her tongue when she was shocked to glance to her left and see Percy looking pale and deflated, chin pointed at the floor, arms at her sides.

"That ain't fair, Cloyd."

"It's the Lord's truth. When you egg him on, you aid and abet the enemy, letting Satan in where, otherwise, he would have no purchase. Now please be quiet and eat. We have company."

To Maggie's surprise, the woman hung her head. During the stunned silence, Maggie realized the spot where Percy had touched her cheek was cooling, as if rubbed by alcohol. After a moment, Cloyd spoke.

"Margaret, how is your daddy? George is my good friend, and I miss seeing him."

"Well, he's—" Maggie needed to cough and clear her throat before continuing. "He's doing . . . better now that he's in . . . a good facility."

It was Cloyd's turn to show surprise. "He's in a nursing home?"

Glad to change the subject, Maggie summarized what had happened since Cloyd had carried her father up to the Big Woods last October. When she described her father's wish to return someday to the cabin, Cloyd laid down his knife and fork to listen, nodding and occasionally shaking his head.

"So I screwed the job up for Dad . . . for you," she finished. "It was a big mistake not to come down here myself to see that the trees were cut correctly. I owe all of you more than an apology, more than . . . receipts. I should take down the cabin and remove all sign we were here."

She longed to be contradicted, but not even the child said anything for the longest time. She wanted Cloyd, she realized (not without some self-disgust), to defend her again. But the deep shame of what she'd done was dissolving her flimsy hope based on little more than her attraction— for she knew she was becoming infatuated with the big man sitting at the end of the table, even if he did pray long prayers and believe in quaint ideas like devils and angels.

She wished she hadn't agreed to this meal and had simply driven back to Dayton, never broken bread where she had no business. Well, she would still do that, as soon as she could politely get away. Her father would want her to see this through, not eat and run, even help clean up, if they'd let her. She would do no more harm to her father's legacy among these people.

"Don't leave. Stay here."

Maggie smiled at the girl. It was the first thing she'd said since being shushed. Before Maggie could respond, Lily left her chair, ran around the table, and climbed into Maggie's lap, hugging her around the neck. The child weighed hardly anything, and, once again eyeing the plate Percy had filled for her, Maggie understood why. She smelled like new-mown grass and clay. Maggie wasn't prepared for how the child felt in her arms. She felt right, snuggling against Maggie's breasts as if she belonged there.

"Thank you, sweetie, but it's best if I go."

"No, no, no! Stay!" She was crying now.

Maggie found her throat closing, her eyes burning, and when she glanced over the girl's shoulder at Cloyd, she saw he had his head bowed, hands tented again. Praying that she'd leave or stay? Percy was no help. Her face was blank, emotionless—a mask? With her own face no longer flushed with heat, Maggie found herself able to think with greater clarity than she had since arriving on The Ridge. She was on her own here in this new land she'd inadvertently despoiled—and continued to despoil with her presence. There was no husband to consult; her father, in his current mental state, could not help her; and Jared, her only friend, inhabited a different galaxy. Therefore, she could hardly believe the words that came out of her mouth.

"We'll see, honey. We'll see." It's what her grandmother used to say when she could not bear to say no to her granddaughter. (*Coward*, Maggie thought, clinging to Lily for dear life.)

Cloyd pushed his chair back and stood. "You can go home now, Percy."

The woman rose as if it were normal to be dismissed like a servant, although Maggie wasn't fooled. She knew the woman was more, much more. (The brother's *wife*—that was it! But . . . it sounded like the brother lived *here*.)

"I got to clean up." Percy reached for the child's plate full of cold food.

EVERY RIVER ON EARTH

"I'd like to do that," Maggie protested.

"No." It was Cloyd's voice of stone. "I'll do it. Margaret, you are our guest. We'll see you tomorrow, Percy."

Removing her apron and hanging it on her chair-back, Percy stepped behind Lily, bent and kissed the top of her head, and was gone. In the silence left after the front door closed behind her, Maggie breathed in the quiet. And relief. The woman had bad karma, Jared would've said; she had, however, made it more comfortable to be in the room with this man who alternately attracted and repelled her. He could go hot to cold, soft to hard in a moment. It was as thrilling as it was intimidating. She stood, picked up her plate, and headed for the sink, considering whether to drive home or spend another night in the cabin. At the window, she looked into the darkness, thankful she couldn't make out the devastation on up the hill. If she left now, she could make it home before midnight.

"I was hoping, Margaret," he said behind her, "that, while I clean up, you might put Lily Clair to bed."

So early? And with hardly any dinner eaten? When Maggie turned, one look at the girl, who'd gone back to palming her clay—plus the memory of her outdoor smell and the feel of her against her chest—was all it took.

"I'd be glad to."

"There's something I want to say to you when you're finished."

When she looked at him, he was studying his hands.

The child's bedroom was another time and place. Once inside, Lily handed Maggie a worn copy of the Golden Classic *Cinderella*, just like the one her own mother had read to her. After the child changed into a long, worn flannel gown, Maggie sat beside her on the bed. While she read, she felt the small body edge closer and closer until her head lay against Maggie's chest. If she'd allowed it, the feeling would've become pity, but she fought it. The child was obviously much less mature than a six-year-old in the suburbs, her behavior more like the five-year-olds she's been around. *But you're not in the 'burbs, Maggie.* And to think what this child lost so recently ...

George's daughter.

The memory of what the girl called her filled her chest with helium; she had to concentrate to keep her voice steady. But teacher defenses kicked in: she would be what this moment and situation required of her. Letting a motherless girl-child cuddle up to her was something she could do. But she would not romanticize it and pretend it was more than what it was. In that way she kept tears out of her voice and things were going fine until Lily reached up, grasped one of Maggie's hands and squeezed it between her own warm, clay-smelling ones. Continuing to read, with difficulty, she felt something moist and warm, looked down and saw the child, fast asleep, had Maggie's thumb in her mouth.

She stopped reading, closed her eyes and let herself feel the stirring deep inside her, a sort of ache, expanding into her lungs and even rising into her throat, taking her breath. Pain or joy, she couldn't tell which, probably both. Lying against the child, she let it work on her until it finally settled to an ember glow. It reminded her of feelings she had early on, after Mark left, when she woke to find herself hugging his pillow after dreaming again he'd been holding her, stroking her stomach, forehead, breasts . . .

"*Margaret.*"

She snapped awake to see Cloyd standing in the doorway. Rising immediately, she covered the girl, whose breathing stayed steady, and followed him into the room he'd earlier called the parlor, a small, dark room lit only by a dim table lamp.

"Please set a minute, if you would."

Part of her resisted—it had been possibly the longest day of her life—but she was curious to hear what he wanted to say. Probably that she should not tear the cabin down. She sat.

"Bless you for staying," he began, sitting in the chair beside her. "And for your kindness to the little 'un. She loves you."

"I don't think—"

"Besides her mama, she has never taken to another female the way she did to you. Poor thing was only four when Anna Lee passed." He bowed his head. "Three years ago."

"But . . . Percy?"

He lowered his eyes for a long moment, then lifted his chin, refocused his gaze. "Percy's mighty good to Lily Clair. Truth is, she's too good, maybe. Makes the girl back off a mite."

His candor emboldened her. "Who is Percy, exactly, I mean, in relation . . ."

"She's Anna Lee's—my wife's—sister."

Ah. A kaleidoscopic barrage of meaning and feelings rushed in. No wonder the woman had been so hostile. This man had put her, Maggie, between a surrogate mama bear and her cub. Sitting forward, Cloyd reached and took her hand from where it hovered at her cheek.

"Dear Margaret, it has not been good here for some time."

I can see that, Maggie felt tempted to but did not say. So why didn't he just let Percy be mama bear? What did it mean that she's *too good?*

"And now you have come."

"Cloyd, it hardly seems that—"

"I need to tell you the truth about me."

"Oh, but you don't owe me—"

"But I want to."

She was struck dumb. His face, what she could see in the dim light, was a study in tenderness. Gone was the harsh lord of the manor. He still held her hand.

"First, I do not have to forgive you for cutting those trees. It's not my place, and, anyway, it's the Lord's vengeance on me. You may think me a saint. I am no saint. I was a logger for ten years, until a tree fell on me and crushed my fibula. Now I'm foreman at the sawmill. I turn those trees you and your daddy love so much into boards for the Amishmen to make these." He touched the table on which the lamp stood.

"Cloyd, I—"

"Second, I am thirty-three years old, and I need a wife."

The room tilted—and Cloyd changed into an old-timey sepia portrait of a man from the last century holding the hand, perhaps caressing the fingers, of his mail-order bride with a calloused, farmer's hand. In addition to his beard, he wore side-whiskers, a vest and jacket from Civil War times. Maggie blinked, and she was back in George Herbert Bush's America, with the New Millennium only a decade away, knee to knee with a twentieth-century sawyer from Marshall County, Ohio, a man born and raised here on Bachelor Ridge.

"I…I…"

She knew she must look like a mental patient. Releasing her hand, Cloyd sat back in the chair and let his chin fall forward till his beard touched his red flannel shirt.

"Forgive me. You must think I have taken leave of my senses. I do feel crazy, a little. But when I laid eyes on you up at the cabin this morning—"

"And I looked like a wreck!"

He tented his fingers as he'd done earlier. Was he about to pray? But he grinned, and immediately looked ten years younger.

"I used to watch you drop George off up at the cabin."

"You could see us from that far away?"

He smiled. "One time I was chopping some wood for him out back of the cabin when I heard the car coming and just stopped—"

"To eavesdrop!" He looked so stricken, she smiled and patted his arm.

"Well, I would have spoken up, but you-all were fussing, and I didn't want to intrude."

She recalled the day exactly, so rarely did she and her father quarrel. He'd insisted on bringing down the chainsaw, saying he was just going to clean it. "I had to make him promise me not to climb trees and cut limbs." She shook her head. "My father didn't like restrictions."

Cloyd's eyes were far away. "What I remember is seeing you up close, before you followed your father into the cabin. I . . . I thought you were beautiful. Now I've seen you at table, I *know* you're beautiful."

For once, the warmth felt good in her cheeks. Still, she was so grateful for the darkness so he couldn't see her flush. Flattering as it all was, though, she needed to stop this fantasy before it went further.

"Cloyd, it's—"

"More important, I saw what a good heart you have, Margaret. Your face, your voice, your actions, all said how much you respect your daddy."

"Thank you, Cloyd, but . . . you don't know me."

His gaze was level, unstinting, as if he saw inside her. "But I do. I know everything I need to know about you."

"You don't. You can't after only—"

"I know you're George Wright's daughter. You have a good soul, and you do not judge."

Us, he didn't say. A flash of insight: that's why Percy had been so hostile at first: she'd expected the outsider to judge, condemn. Despite her trembling fingers and the ocean roaring in her ears, Maggie found her resistance waning. This good man's approval felt good; no, better than that: it felt wonderful. It was something she hadn't had in a long, long time. But, nice as it was, it was still fantasy, and, to save them both, she determined not to listen any more.

"Cloyd, I'm nine years older than you. I'm a divorcee whose husband left her because she couldn't have children and . . ." The instant flush left her too breathless to add, *and many, many other flaws.*

"I have a child," he said, nodding gravely toward his daughter's room. "I need no more."

Maggie resisted the urge to turn toward Lily's door. Yes, her heart had let in the child who needed a mother—and so much more than Maggie in her barrenness, her preoccupation with herself, could provide. But she was shocked to even be considering why she couldn't be this man's wife! Had the events of this strange day somehow charmed her into somnolence? But she wasn't completely hypnotized; Maggie saw clearly that Cloyd meant to place her squarely between Percy and her niece.

There was no way. The thought calmed her. Wait till she told Jared when she got home! He would realize the seriousness and not make fun. Now that she understood this conversation could not lead anywhere, she allowed herself to take her host's hand and squeeze it. She could be less guarded, now that she'd decided it was all a dream.

"Lily Clair is beautiful," she began, "and you are very sweet to open your home to a stranger." He started to speak but she held a finger to his lips, oddly feeling in control, now her real life was back in the room. "But I have a dying father who needs me."

When Cloyd dropped his head, Maggie's heart skittered a little. She'd of course been enjoying the fantasy. Still . . .

"I have a lot of decisions to make about what's best for him, what to tell him as his body and mind go. And I'll be returning to teaching in just a few days." She laughed. "I'm an old woman, Cloyd, and a city slicker and persnickety, too." She hated that word; it was Mark's. The last thing she needed was him here.

At last Cloyd looked up, tired but not defeated. "Anna Lee was a strong woman, too, God rest her soul."

Maggie found herself tearing up again. How could she not? The man had suffered, was suffering. And the tears were for herself, too. Plus, it was getting crowded with both of their former spouses, her father, and best friend now in the room. Plus, there were photographs, the older ones black and white, of long-dead ancestors, no doubt. Maggie avoided their eyes.

"But you think me a widow-man just wanting a stand-in for his deceased wife. That's not it, Margaret. I know you, and you are not her. You are only yourself."

She saw that he meant it, even believed it, though of course he was deluded. But something was pulling her back into the seductive fantasy of marriage to this hill native, as if the very walls of this house, or the ground on which it stood, exuded a sort of magnetism, a will of its own, whispering: Come home. But home was hours away, in suburban Dayton, Ohio.

"Then tell me one thing you know about me that my father didn't tell you."

He didn't hesitate. "You're every bit as strong as your mama was, and her mama before her."

It jolted up her spine. She realized that both her mother and grandmother had been with her this whole day, standing behind her chair as; they had passed her the gravy, telling her when to speak, when to hush. And not to judge. She was powerless to prevent the tear rolling down her cheek.

Instantly Cloyd pulled a white handkerchief from his shirt pocket and handed it to her. It smelled like sheets hung outside in a stiff breeze. (Had the man known he'd need a clean hankie tonight? The thought, like the man, both comforted and disturbed.)

"Thank you, I'm . . . I'm sorry."

She wiped her eyes, remembering what she hadn't in a long time. Those years her mother had lingered after the cancer diagnosis, as her body began slowly breaking down, turning against her, until at last she was in a wheelchair, then bedridden.

"I'll see you graduate," her mother had said, though Maggie was a college sophomore when she got sick; but she had. When Maggie fell in love with Mark Absher in junior year, her mom had said, "I'll be there with your father to give you away." Maggie hugged her and knew it was impossible. But she'd been there, in her wheelchair, breathing oxygen, and had even stayed until halfway through the reception, during which George, dear George, had never left her side.

No Kentucky relatives were invited, of course (the grandparents dead by this time), but Maggie didn't care. Her mama had chosen Maggie's "uppity" Catholic father, and if that meant no kinfolk at her wedding, that was fine. But here in this country house far from the city (in the third world, Jared would say), she felt the price her mother had paid for choosing her father. Did that make her mother strong or weak?

"Margaret?"

It was Cloyd calling her back.

"I'd like to walk you home before my brother gets home. He can be orn'ry when he's drunk. Lily Clair's a heavy sleeper. She won't know a thing till her uncle gets in."

Maggie felt rescued once more. She hadn't answered his question, but, despite her relief, she felt a surge of disappointment, too. Would he ask again?

"No," she said rising. "I need to go up there alone tonight." When he started to rise, she put both hands on his shoulders, and he let her force him to keep his seat. Then, glancing at the ancestors' photos and quickly turning away, she kissed the top of his head (remembering how Percy had done the same to Lily) and walked toward the door. Had she fled quickly, she might've escaped, but something made her pause just as her hand reached to push the screen open. Where was the brother? She had a sudden image of him outside listening. But they'd heard no vehicle, and she presumed he wouldn't arrive on foot.

"Maggie." That big granite voice curling around the doorframe from the parlor to catch her almost to the threshold made her freeze. "You will consider my offer."

Only later, lying on the cot trying to sleep, would Maggie recall it had not been a question.

JANET LADRACH

The Farmer's Wife's Vacation

Says Ruby to Erleen, "Me and the ole man took our vacation yesterday."

"Oh yeah?" she says, "What did you do?"

"Well, after he fed calves and milked the cows
and kinda looked everything over,
he come on back to bed."

"You're kiddin'!"

"No I ain't. Then we had us a little 'vo-de-oh-do' and
then we went out to breakfast.
I had me some of that French toast with berries."

"Was it good?"

"Yep. We're goin' again next year."

Watching My Neighbor in His Fields

All the long morning, T-shirts, jeans blessed
over and over with sweat. My farmer
neighbor's an aging barber busy grooming
his fields, endless lines of rustling grass.

Below hay mist and puffs of yellow confetti,
the tractor pulls, August heat drags him.
He holds on. It's a test of wills, forcing stuff
to pack up and go; even grass knows it has

a voice. At dusk, he leans against fence rails,
fingers folded chews grass like a used straw.
In evening air, bunnies and mice run over his body
it lies yonder under the tractor's thrum.

And he's thrown his son into summer,
the deep blue end of its days, taught him
the hand ballet of its combs and scissors.
Looking forward, looking back, he cuts,

binds and loads. One eye on his mirror,
the other on the sky. Swim or sink, grass
is just another word for boys,
and they'll wrestle when caught for a trim.

The price of milk's down; all his sheds
are on their knees, still he brings us sweet
corn, plows our driveway for free. I shake
my head. Later, after calves get watered,

get fed, without grumbling, the farmer's son
swings himself to the tractor's seat,

tines pass over the fields easy as a broom.
He hums and whistles as he sweeps

his father's floor. For almost nothing,
he cleans the church.

JULIE L. MOORE

A Clear Path

He drives his red truck to the field,
the farmer who once ran into our mailbox, saying,
You people and your big houses git in the way.

This harvest day, from our window,
my son and I watch him and his pal stretch
tape measure from a fence post, then a road sign,

to our mailbox across the way. They nod at one another,
hop back into his Chevy. A good ol' boy telepathy.
Then he pulls into our drive, reverses in a straight line,

rams the gold-and-black sign, throwing caution
to the ground. We blink in disbelief as he grabs
a chainsaw from the back, rips

through the base of the post in five seconds flat.
And drives away,
kicking up our confusion with the gravel.

I once wrote about a vulture that perched
on that post. Both are gone now.
A clear path often means loss.

And within minutes, his combine emerges
like a realization, turns the corner, skirts
past my mailbox, lowers its enormous blade,

and plows into the grain like a tidal wave.

The Way Things Are

Summer Solstice, 2010

Last night I saw my neighbor throw
one leg over a corner of the moon.

He must have ridden it like that,
cowboy style, all night long.

I didn't see him again until dawn,
when he came whistling up the street,

slapping moon dust from his jeans.
He must have slid down onto a rooftop,

the way a short man leaves a tall horse.
He tipped his hat, said *Morning, ma'am,*

but the dog just stood there, straight
legged and still, the way she does

when she knows something that I do not.
I served him coffee in my best china cup,

watched him lift it to his weathered face,
saw the coffee eclipse the cup, rise

and then fall back again upon itself,
the way night overtakes the day,

smooth and deliberate, with no hint
of remorse or explanation. He talked

about the weather, the lack of rain,
what drought was doing to his garden,

but his eyes stopped me from asking
what I wanted to know about moonlight

and darkness. He just drained the cup
chucked the dog under her chin,

whispered into her dark ear, *That's just
the way things are . . . just the way they are.*

JEANNE BRYNER

August 1976:
Bertha Welcomes Me to the Neighborhood

A sweet voice calls
from the screen door's other side.

Her apron's alive, blooms buttercups.
Just as short as my grandmother, she
wears her plain gray hair, sensible
shoes, a white slip under her dress.

In her arms, twin zucchini, ripe
tomatoes, squash. Like a sleeping
baby, she cradles them.
Near a tangled path
of boxes, I stumble
over words, chew gum.

I'm surprised when she asks
about my washer, our well,
Automatics take a lot of water—
be careful—
(she points to my kitchen floor)
this here's a hand-dug well.

Her tone lifts my chin
I try to swallow the gum,
Yes ma'am, I reply, sliding
down inside my skin
the only desk I've got.

Bertha, please forgive the lateness
of my note, I believe

extraordinary
is the word I tried to find
the day you came
saying, *Honey, just sit down*
for work won't go away.
Thanks for a full afternoon
of your stories, they still
taste like warm berry pie
    with sugar-sprinkled crust
        kindness carried forward
            on your way to the moon.

Outside

Stevie lives in a silo.
A silo lives where, mostly, Stevie is
or is not. Tipped over—a hollow vein.
The silo, I mean. For here home is out
there on the grass. If you want a drink or wash
your hands, just dip into that trunk, hot and cold
running branches feeding down. It's startling.
But sense is startling too. See how those boots
flip skyward? Tongues lapping up dew on his
mache dandelions. This is Stevie's dream

mini-acreage on the family's old spread.
He's all spread out, he's humming when he makes
a working thing—he won't let you inside.
So, he says. Today he's stacked two propane
tanks and ovens—two-burners—under a
red maple and when you open a door
there's mismatched silver and hatchets and things
he's made to eat *and* art with. Studio
as wherever-you're-itching-at-the-time:
boards with big nails banged in and from the nails

hang gourds, baby-sized cups spackled yellow
(is that old egg?), a hundred kinds of who
knows what, the center being where you are
and are not. I stay dry, he says. No bugs.
Says, why do walls want windows? He's put glass
around his trees instead, head-high to look
at trees from outside out. One chair, sleeping bag
—what he keeps inside his wild corn bin—

plus a getaway, by which he means a tunnel.
Oh oh, he says, they coming. He can worm

his way all the way to the apple trees.
He trenched it out last fall and lights the route
with flashlights and tinfoil clipped to clothesline.
That's a trip. And that's a curvy planter full
of nursery nipples and hand-dipped Ken dolls.
If you want to see one art made wholly
in an outside mind, come see Stevie's crib.
That's his ten-foot pink polyvinyl penis
teeter-totter beside the birdcage
for tomatoes. Take a ride, he says. All eyes.

BENJAMIN S. GROSSBERG

In Memoriam: Ginger

Ginger, whom I did not like to look at, or talk to, to whom
I was polite only by an act of will, is dead, dead and gone.
Vacant now: her apartment, the only one in the basement—
by the laundry and the small storage cubbies that the landlord
throws in free. I saw the ambulance, noticed it a few weeks ago
when I shut my lights for sleep: blue and red flashing
through the blinds. I looked out to see Ginger's daughter—
apartment three, other side of the building—walk doggedly
back and forth on the lawn, from her apartment door back out
to the curb. I didn't know then it was for Ginger. Ask not.
That knowledge came later, when I told Aline—first floor,
decorates the hall for Christmas, Easter, the seasons generally,
plastic snowflakes, that sort of thing—that she looked nice.
Aline said it was for Ginger, the funeral held earlier that morning.

I wondered why I hadn't been invited, but then I remembered
that Aline is kind to everyone, and I, a snob, had rejected Ginger.

My difficulty with Ginger wasn't due to her weird body,
though that bothered me, her weird breasts hanging down nearly
to her waist. I'm not saying this was her fault. Or her laugh—
I want to write "cackle"—how loud it was, how I could see
when she laughed that her teeth were cracked, blackened,
that her middle-aged gums had burned-out spaces.
The landlord once tried to evict Ginger for having a cat.
The whole building was up in arms because others had cats, too.
I'm the only tenant with a dog; I didn't get involved.
Even though the entire basement—laundry area, cubbies—
smelled like her catbox, the landlord eventually relented.

38   EVERY RIVER ON EARTH

But none of this especially disturbed me about Ginger.
Certainly not enough to hope she'd be forced to leave.

No, the problem was her speech. The way she spoke
sent my shoulders up, made me back away nearly instinctively,
as from an object that cast my own humanity into doubt. Ginger
slurred her words incredibly, tortured and twisted each word
out of her mouth, each syllable like Blake's tyger, violently
hammered in the furnace of her gullet. At first I thought
it was an Ohio drawl, but the more I heard it—scraping
chalkboards sonorous by comparison—the more I realized
it was all Ginger and no Ohio. I'd never heard anyone
do that to language before: no alcohol, no organic instigation
that I could see, just Ginger opening her mouth hugely,
gaping her mouth like a cavern at dusk delivering a nearly
unending stream of bats—the deep, cavernous mouth
guarded by only a few shards of teeth. It was horrible.
I kept my eyes down on the washer when she spoke,
my hands on the machine as if feeling for psychic contact
with the laundry. I didn't understand a word she said.

I thought to ask Pat—second floor, across the hall from me,
clutters the area outside her door with boxes of scarves—
how Ginger died. Pat wouldn't judge me for asking,
even though it's not my business. Or is it? These people
with whom I live, whose sounds I know nearly as well
as my own—whose business if not mine? The woman
whose living room abuts my bedroom: I know what she sings
to help her baby sleep. She knows the universe
of pet names I have for my dog. What could be more
embarrassing than that? No more awkwardly intimate
or unchosen than those people into whom I was born,
though here with the surprising element of tolerance—

except for Ginger, whom I did not tolerate, unless avoidance
too is a brand of tolerance, maybe tolerance's last resort.

Benjamin S. Grossberg

Ginger's door has been left open; she died midmonth,
so her clothes, her things have the space a few more weeks.
After that someone new will come, and with or without effort,
that person will know and become known—will enlarge
this thing that isn't a family, that is both more and less
than friendship, our daily unacknowledged intimacy. How odd
that it could be anyone. But that's for later. Now, the apartment
is still Ginger's, the empty space a collective—if temporary—
testament to her memory. I can see quite clearly inside,
her things half packed in boxes for Goodwill, the undusted
closed blinds. Almost nothing, finally, of whatever it is
that Ginger was: mother and tenant, I guess; maker,
if nothing else, of a sound that has vanished from the world.

DIANE KENDIG

Written on a Big Cheap Postcard
From the James Wright Festival in Martins Ferry, Ohio, 1999

We are nothing but a poet's dream
Of lovers who choose to live.
                                        —James Wright

I drove here on NPR fund-raising day,
the Shostakovich *Hamlet* film score playing,
sixteen singers singing,
"The moon shines bright. In such a night as this,
when the sweet wind did gently kiss the trees
and they did make no noise,"
but now at 5 am at the Red Roof Inn,
there is noise the third time since 11 pm from the men
in room 249 who pound their door and shout, "Police!"

Awake the whole six hours in room 247, I want
to scream, "Will you shut up, you assholes?"
which is not poetic, as everything
in Martins Ferry is every year on these three days,
and "Yes, I bite my thumb at you" no longer
offends anyone. I try, "I bite my thumb at you,
you assholes," but think better, think

how you'd open the door the first time
and say, "Will you please stop?" so mildly
the two would have to pause to hear you,
then fists raised, midair, collapsing on their wrists,
and wide-eyed as those somnambulists Trinculo and Stefano,
led forward by the final strains of reconciliation,

they would trip into their own door, yawning,
and everyone could sleep, dear Prospero.

Now hark, what light through yonder window breaks?
The real police glide up under my balcony
and the pounders scurry indoors.
Wishing you were here, glad for you you're not.

Remembering James Wright

I see you in a coal barge tugged
upriver to Wheeling, or
tossing back boilermakers, spirit of Li Po
possessing you, ruptured night watchman
on the next barstool.

Now you mull varieties,
subtleties of hangovers,
reworking a poem about wasted lives as
the branch outside your window breaks
into blossom.

Born a hundred slag piles east,
a generation later,
I too longed to stoke the heart's open hearth,
forge song from labors' sweat-soaked oaths,
commune with the ancient
Chinese governor stepping over
a mud puddle

I too longed to embrace the moon
reflected in your Ohio.

TWO

THE LAND

Ohio Hills

They move—I know they do:

on days as clear as honest eyes,

or in a steeping fog,

they hold their breath

till I pretend to sleep,

then gather up their goods

like bundled ladies on a bus,

in window seats

away from some cigar.

Beside Spring Creek
(Ohio River Valley Watershed)

The dog and I have sat so long beside the creek,
suspended between the reflected world
and the one above,

that we can no longer tell the difference between
the shimmer of the water and the gleam
of a September sky.

The sycamores' white branches thread their way
along the creek bottom where the dog hunts
the nether world,

neither here nor there, watching for crayfish stilled
by the autumn chill, or . . . yes . . . for a squirrel
that will make the leap

from one familiar limb to another. Trusting his own
lucky instincts, he plunges into the stream.
The water rocks

with the explosion, the sun rippling like a pennant.
But with no scent to follow he gives up the chase,
returns to the bank,

wet, but not discouraged. It was not an illusion; he does
not feel tricked. It's simply the way things are—
like the face that I see

in the watery shadows, the hand on my shoulder,
warm and familiar, that causes me to look up,
even when there is no one there.

No one has followed us to this place, but the touch
is real if I want it to be, and may be real
even if I do not.

Someday, the sycamores ...

... are going to pick up their roots
and walk away, but for now they are waiting
for the young ones to grow legs.

It is a slow, but inevitable process. Still, danger inches
closer every year. There is the creek, and the bank,
and, of course, the road

and the railing which keeps the road from tumbling
into the creek. Danger is slow but ever present,
and they are watchful.

Any season it might be necessary to raise the alarm.
Some will undoubtedly be left behind—the old,
the very young,

those who live so close to the edge that there is no hope
of their safe return. Still, the sun shines, they stretch
and grow, years pass.

Some fall in love with rocks and will not be budged;
others are in debt to the wind, but all worship
the sun that urges them upward,

all elbows and knees and crooked joints, climbing
some invisible ladder that gives them courage
to try the impossible.

When the ice melts, and the stream rushes forward,
undermining roots, lifting boulders like tombstones,
they know it is time.

And if you watch carefully, if you sit down in the dark
when the moon, that old tattletale, is out of sight,
you will see them stand

on gnarled knuckles and inch away, see them gather up
their children, hand in hand, and even if you call,
they will not turn back.

RICHARD HAGUE

Sycamore Country

It's less than a ten-minute walk from here, not far away at all from the rap-hammering, traffic-conduiting, long-suffering heart of Madisonville. I walk down littered Erie Ave., go left past the dusty piles of the Stone Center, out onto Madison Road loud with traffic, past the Speedway gas station and the dudes gassing their hoopties in the lot, trunk-rattling woofers drumming and vibrating. I pass my wife's former studio, which has stood these many years empty and ugly since her slumlord doubled the rent, saying, "I've got lots of people just waiting to take it," and then went on to trash the whole place. "It's only Madisonville," his attitude groused. "Who cares how shabby it looks? Who cares about its land?" He filled the side yard with vehicles, dumped a load of gravel over the lawn in the other side lot, and left piles of broken glass and debris on the sidewalk in front. When we saw it all coming, my wife and I hurried up there and dug out a few of the vintage peony bushes that had grown in the backyard since the time of the Lammers family's habitation on the land. A week later, dump trucks were parked over the holes we had hastily filled in. What makes it all the worse is that those of us who have taken the time to learn a little local history and so try to align our minds as well as our senses to where we live, know that the building he is treating thusly is one of the oldest in Madisonville, the site of the first general hardware store here, built by the Lammers family with bricks made of clay dug on the site. It's a paragon of the local, even its materials arising literally out of its place. Generations of Lammers are buried in the Laurel Hill Cemetery, six blocks from here. To see this history obliterated by some arrogant parvenu is doubly offensive. He even nagged the city until they removed the Urban Forestry trees they had planted on Madison Road. I pass all that, cursing him, then turn left, check out the oncoming traffic, and make my move to cross over to Camargo Road. A couple of hundred paces north, past tiny houses leashed to barking dogs, I walk beyond where the sidewalk ends. I step onto the weedy shoulder, turn a gentle curve, and am out of sight of the city.

For nearly a mile, the road could be anywhere in a thousand places in Appalachia. I have to crane my neck and look deliberately up to see any sky; the road skirts the creek, which crosses beneath the pavement through a concrete culvert the size of a railroad tunnel, and which my younger son Brendan discovered as a boy and adventured in for days with his friends. The hillsides of the winding hollow through which the creek runs are steep and densely wooded, and along the rocky banks, huge sycamores glow white, this time of the year, against brown tree trunks and the umbers and sienas of the forest duff. One is especially elegant, rising forty feet before its first branching, and the pattern its pale limbs make against the background of the hillside, I suddenly realize, is the pattern for the stylized trees I have drawn all my life. Their branches always start out from the trunk almost perfectly horizontal, then suddenly rush up, creating squarish frames of white in which segments of blue sky gleam like lenses. There is something hypnotic to me about this pattern. I repeat it and repeat it and repeat it; early on, the sycamore entered my consciousness with a kind of visual fury, and its architecture was burned indelibly into me, becoming the archetype of all trees.

My late friend Joe Enzweiler, who grew up in the village this road leads to, used to take me on sycamore hunts. In his drives through the country-side looking for "bullrock" with which to build the beautiful walls at his brother's homestead in Campbell County, Kentucky, he'd discover huge sycamores, invariably along a creek, down in a hollow, each tree larger or more ponderous than the last. He'd make a note of the location, and then some winter Saturday, he'd take me there, and we'd stand near its trunk and snap a photo or two, and casually admire its size and its wild beauty. Men and great trees have always stood next to one another thus; there exist hundreds of photos taken everywhere from Eastern Kentucky's virgin white oak slopes in the nineteenth century to the stiffly posed lumberjacks and pilgrims in the Pacific Northwest's redwood groves. If, as Melville says, "water and meditation are wedded forever," there is also some kindred union between humans and trees, though too often involving the former's destruction of the latter.

I imagine that sycamores were tourist attractions even back in pioneer days, before the first Brambles and Whetsels and Muchmores and Stiteses settled in this neck of the woods and who, upon dying, gave their names to the streets of my village. A big sycamore is a landscape event. It is so visible in its place that it can be used to give directions—"Walk up the creek until the third big sycamore on your left—the one with the hollow trunk—then climb the hill directly to the ridgetop. Look west and you'll see my house." When I summered in southeastern Ohio during my premature midlife crisis almost forty years ago, I occasionally visited a little town called Sycamore Corners, where there was a general store, a gas pump, and a creek. The sycamores edged the stream like a procession of white-robed deacons. Sitting there, I felt more than the usual need to keep in line. And of course a tree with the size some sycamores achieve can even, if one is pressed hard enough, provide a dwelling for a season.

There's a huge old sycamore in Lindner Park, off Indian Mound Avenue, in Norwood, a few miles from here. I visited it once and felt like a pilgrim; I lingered around its sprawling base as one would linger in the precincts of a European cathedral, trying to imagine the past, wondering what creatures may have overnighted or overwintered in its dim enclosure.

As I walked Camargo Road in the presence of these sycamores, I was also in the presence of the creek itself, with its variable voice, its multiple songs. There is a four-foot cataract near where the creek exits the culvert, and as is usually the case, below it stretches a deep long pool. The water cascades into it with a musical rush, and I think of it as a kind of aural shrine, a pastoral counterpoint to the urban crash left behind, and in its quiet I linger.

We in the city who need these moments and these relatively undomesticated vistas have to practice what the poet John Keats called "negative capability," which involves living patiently with contradiction. Instead of wrangling with ourselves over the mess and ugliness of the city as set against the natural countryside, wishing we could have more of the one and less of the other, we have to be able to simply close our spirits' eyes as we pass through the ugly, and open them on the beautiful. Little beyond a kind of short-lived catharsis can come of railing against the litter, the Mad Dog bottles in the gutter, the sloth and greed of slumlords, the stink and honk of traffic. We are given what we are given, and though I am not advocating passivity in the face of that which attacks our spirit and our sensibilities, neither am I advocating constant dissatisfaction. This enervates us, and renders us unfit for our necessary battles against meanness and ignorance and hostility. We still have to endure the Community Council meeting, crammed with the frequently inconsequential but nevertheless unignorable crises of neighborhood democracy; we still have to make the irate phone call to the proper city agencies or to the police; we still have to take time out to draft the letter to the housing inspector or the county engineer. But we cannot allow ourselves to be nagged to death by these things; we have to enjoy what we can, in its time.

So I hike Camargo Road, or whatever region of solitude and beauty I can find within walking distance of my home. The Laurel Cemetery nearby on Roe Street affords a pleasant silence, a few large trees, though nothing near as admirable as the Camargo sycamores, and to the almost-elderly saunterer and reader of headstones, a quiet reminder, as if he needed it, of mortality.

And if I were to live where there are no such places, I think I would feel a bit diminished. I would have to ask myself such questions as, "Is it acceptable that the only place I can go for leaves and shadows and the sound of water is a place I must drive to, adding pollution to the very thing I want to preserve?" Or, "Remembering Thoreau's observation that the cost of a thing is how much life I must give up in order to obtain it, how much is my peace costing me? How much is it costing the environment? Is there some way to live more gently and more lightly on the land, so that I do not cost it its peace and wholeness?" Or, "Am I content with the fact that my children interact with video games more intently than they study the intricate and varied world of nature around us? Is it appropriate that they know better how to blast an enemy on 'Grand Theft Auto' than how to attract a hummingbird to our yard? Do I have any neighbors who keep a record of the weather?"

One cold day several winters ago, a glaze of ice covering everything, I was walking toward the cemetery when I heard a loud pounding beyond and above me, as if someone were working on a roof. As I scanned the houses, I caught a sudden movement in the top of an old silver maple along a side street. It was an astounding sight to me—first, because I knew exactly what I was seeing, and second, because it was the last thing I expected to see in the city. It's called the Pileated woodpecker, and I first saw one as a boy in the woods of Wayne National Forest, in the hills of Appalachian Ohio. Now I was looking at one less than two blocks from my house, in the middle of a neighborhood better known for its rappers and car-repair joints than for its wildlife.

What a treasure it was to see such a thing that day. I wanted to rush around to my neighbors, pounding on their doors and crying out the good bird news to them, or to hustle my own kids out of doors for a once-in-a-lifetime sighting, but I knew I'd likely embarrass them. Still, the presence of that animal in my neighborhood, like the presence of the sycamores and their quiet creekside so nearby, was news more important than is covered on most of TV. It revived something in me that otherwise might have continued to decline for the rest of the long darkness of winter. I have looked again for it each time I walk that way, but no luck. Though the bird's presence fades to dream and memory, it is already the central point of a story I will tell and tell, hallowing in words its epiphany in this unlikely place.

Not Children

I know. But let me describe how gently
I pulled apart the plastic, the cowl, how the plastic
split at its stapled seam, revealing wet, olive-
colored bark. I'm not exaggerating when I say
I've never seen anything more beautiful
in the human body, though it did most resemble
human skin. Let me talk about the winnowing
of fingers through barrows of the local clay
cut with composted horse manure, fingers, arms
up to the elbow, sifting, mixing, breaking up
clumps of the compost, feathering it over
heavy clay, aerating, leavening, darkening.
Let me describe the speckled brown:
how the mixed medium had richness, felt good
on the palms, soft on the soft parts of the body.
Now imagine yourself bending with me,
lifting a tree from the plastic, extricating a single
sapling from the bundle, how your fingers
relearn gentleness unlacing the hair of the roots
from other roots, how in the manner of a mother
washing a child, you touch the most vulnerable
parts of the tree, the places where it would be
frighteningly easy to choke off life. And now
let's stand together, lift it from the plastic
and wash it down again, the pressure of the hose
blocked by your palm, so water falls easily
on the young trunk. Its place in the world is prepared;
bring it over, rest it in, as if into human arms.
The earth will love the thing no more than we do.
And now imagine yourself with me
stepping back from the planted sapling. Feel
how you steep and rise, how your chest fills
and then the slow, steady release of air.

Chipmunk a peripheral imposition
afterimage headed into the den beneath
one of the treated six-by-six sills that found
the outhouse
   the eye never catches
up but plots a path to satisfy
that indiscrete stroke traversing
the tangential kiss of what I can say I saw

   *

Twenty years ago red maple saplings wound
around one another bound by
twigs at the top. They have grown
together, an eight-foot trunk of double-heliacal rib standing
up a tree three times that. What might be
made of such a shaft: cured, barked and buffed to light
rose "so hard a cat couldn't scratch" legs for a table but why
surrender that irreplicable extent? Carve a head
on it; add a dedication to the relevant
goddess and a legend:
       Her Nightmare is His Dream
or
   Her Dream is His Nightmare

   *

Walking the creek bed he picked up a siltstone fragment nickel-sized but
shaped like Ohio on the map. Further down a weathered hexagonal bath
tile about three inches across the points. They rubbed together in his pocket
until changing jeans he laid them on the writing desk. The next time its
surface needed cleaned they got tossed into a brass ashtray among projec-
tile points, potsherds, and like curiosities. Mending something weeks later
he noticed the two pieces, dotted the center of the tile with left-over two-
part epoxy and pressed the stone to it, which assemblage stuck around for
thirty-five years, coming into focus every so often out of whatever clutter it

had held subliminally in order. Then he pinned it to the kitchen wall with a pair of roofing nails, its most conspicuous venue in ages of being shaped so long before Ohio was.

Box

How long can things fall apart?

House a crushed bouquet, you come across it decomposing, fourfold form following dysfunction, diagonals working at cross-purposes, mommy, daddy, daughter, son, XYZinfinity
dis

coordinating, an edifice of powder, a nomadic (time-traveling) structure, its corrugated grimace and brick tears cascade over . . .

Shoebox, saltbox, snuffbox, a room . . . boxed set, pine box, ears boxed. Here at the sky end of the box, here at the earth end of the box. That's only the oily circumstances, Jack; no strings barred, no holds attached.

Listing, lists, lines (stout vines) sustaining the lists, all along the sideyards, backyards, yards. Shack, shed, shanty, patched

asunder, rent together; the usual smooth; odorless, opaque.

Live in a box, compose in a box. In the round (just for contrast, for equal time): yurts, tipis, wells, towers, silos, arenas, corncribs, theaters.
—
Houses in ruin . . . Three by five, four by five, six by eight, ten by twelve. Leveled, not level.

Patchpinned, bobbyworked. Makeshifted, jury-rigged.

No room for ghosts, too small for ghosts.

Henhouses, woodsheds, transient quarters. Railroad switch houses, booths, carved initials. Raggedy slats, walleyed windows, guillotine glass.

Pot-glass.

Collecting dust as a hobby, village carpenter on hold.

Hallows Eve
Ohio, 2011

Painted white letters on warped plywood proclaim
THE KINGDOM OF GOD IS AT HAND,
a message lost on the rusted tractor that stands
like a plinth amid cornstalks bent over knee-high.
A recumbent doe spreads her entrails down the berm,
inviting a haruspex's interpretation.
The sinus-clearing tang of polecat in the air.
Branches of a bare maple, like fleshless fingers, greet the shadows.
Hollows filled with tendrils of fog fine as spiderwebs.
The serrated tips of Appalachian ridgebacks
rise above the gray like teeth at the end of October.

Too Many

my neighbors
say, when what they mean
     are deer—the foragers, the few at a time, fair

if little more
than rats, according to
     a farmer friend nearby, whose corn means plenty.

They nip the peaches,
and one bite ruins;
     hazard every road with their running-

into-headlights-
not-away; a
     menace; plague; something should be done.

  Or here in town,
where I've
     found a kind of afterlife—the townies hate

the damage to their varie-
gated hostas,
     shadeside ferns—what they do inside white bunkers of

the county's one good
course is "criminal,"
     deep scuffs through the sand—that's one thing—but

lush piles of polished-
olive droppings, hoof-
     ruts in the chemically and color-enriched greens . . .

    Yet here's
one more, curled
        like a tan seashell not a foot from my blade, just-

come-to-the-
world fawn, speckled,
        wet as a trout, which I didn't see, hacking back

brush beneath my tulip
poplar—it's not afraid,
        mews like a kitten, can't walk: there are so many, too

many of us,
the world keeps saying,
        and the world keeps making—this makes no sense—more.

Cardinals

Just before daybreak
  tweezering at the cold edge
for a disk of sun.

Whipping, whipping air
  out from the poplar in waves:
Here I am, here, here.

Common, loud, garish,
  a pinup in the field guide,
amateurs' first crush.

Flitting jerky-hop
  from twig to twig on the limb—
never the right spot.

A shopkeeper's eye,
  relentless, shutter-quick, honed
on the day's small gains.

Perched on the phonelines
  calling sunset, hooked around
the black rope of talk.

MICHELLE Y. BURKE

Horse Loquela

loquela
... *the flux of language through which the subject tirelessly rehashes the effects of a wound* ...
—Roland Barthes

The horse's eye socket is empty, scraped clean of sight.
A depression in bone. There and not there. A living blank.

His flanks are smooth as leaves swollen with rain, scent rising
like steam. Rain begins, a shudder of skin over bone,
and the ground absorbs it all.

        The socket is velvet-lined,
round like a thumbprint in mud. I place my finger where the eye
should be. No shudder. I don't press, though I want to,
though I always want to.

        Caresses turn. Repetition blisters.

The horse's pulse quickens against my finger.

        Outside, the veins
of the laden sky open, an outpouring.

MICHELLE Y. BURKE

Market Day

The sky is clear tonight. The plow horses
stand silent in the field, and the wife calls
to her husband to bring the truck around:
Tomorrow is market day, and the lettuces
must be packed in the cool night hours.

If their vegetables are beautiful, they can ask
a high price, so they swaddle their lettuces
in burlap and stack the crates carefully.
When the truck is loaded, the wife follows
her husband up the stairs to the bedroom

they'd built to be a hayloft back when
there was still going to be a house. At dawn,
she'll rise and go downstairs and milk
her goats. She'll drive away, leaving behind
for his morning coffee a single jar of milk.

The Poet Performs in the Theater of Cows

There is nothing better, I have decided,
than walking past cows and their calves in their pasture
and watching them watch you like spectators, like fans.
Especially after weeks of multiple rejections
that lead, inevitably, to a wretched state
of dejection. It's downright uplifting, the sight of those eyes
glued to your every move. So I wave. I say hello.
I can't help myself. I am the center
of their attention, here in their open-air theater.

And as they stare, they chew their cud. Which stirs me
to regurgitate a poem no editor seems to want to publish.
A poem I love, mind you. A poem, I'm suddenly convinced,
they'll love, too. I recite aloud every fat and juicy verse
on the stage of my rural road.
I say the words with emphasis,
not the way some poets at public readings lift
the pitch of their monotone voices at the end of each line
like they've somehow gone Scandinavian,
but that kind of thespian emphasis with suspenseful
pauses, eager enunciations. A Shakespearean
kind of performance.

And every brown eye of all these four-legged, slaughter-
bound groundlings is still on me.
Some even stop their masticating, hang
their mouths wide open. Even the young ones,
who had been fidgeting in the field before I came along,
seem mesmerized. I finally have a captive
audience. And when I finish, I leave them
utterly speechless.

Wine Tasting, Nine A.M.

When someone you cannot see whistles
when you weren't expecting, the October orange light
stops still mid-pour through the window.
If you raise your face, you can taste it—notes of maple,
hint of hay, is that the dusty sidewalk just outside?
And the finish—traces of thin clouds filtering
the universe as it comes to us in this town,
leaving discernible flavors. The whistler
knows this. That's why he whistles.

DAVID LEE GARRISON

Every River on Earth

I look out the window and see
through the neighbor's window

to an Amish buggy
where three children are peeping back,

and in their eyes I see the darkness
of plowed earth hiding seed.

Wind pokes the land in winter,
trying to waken it,

and in the melting snow
I see rainbows and in them

every river on earth. I see all the way
to the ocean, where sand and stones

embrace each falling wave
and reach back to gather it in.

THREE

THE GRIND

In Line for the Cashier

I know what it's like to be hungry,
to open the cupboards to find
only broken cockroach legs

and trails of mysterious powder,
and to stand in hesitation
for a moment before I licked

my finger and tested the dust,
hoping for white sugar or salt,
or the muted taste of flour.

I suppose this is what I think
when I see the man with cat food.
He pushes a full shopping cart

with dozens of Fancy Feast cans
to the cashier's till. He bends
to help her fill the plastic sacks.

The young, female cashier recoils
as she opens each sack for the cans,
her hands inside to guide his own in.

Each time this repeats, his head swings
toward her high, round breasts.
She flinches as she tries to do this job.

Everything about him says, *I starve,*
the threadbare corduroys, the knobby wrists
jutting from the second-hand sweater,

and the hollowed, caved-in facial bones,
the last, the telltale sign of one who's lost all
his teeth. This scene demands

silence, a collective witnessing,
of the man's orbit toward her breasts,
her little back-up dance away from him.

In the social decorum of Petco
no one says anything. Not the man
who clutches organic kibble.

Not the woman with the pomeranian
and the squeaky toys. Not the manager.
Not even I know what to say and so say

nothing. As he wobbles toward the exit
with his bags of food on this subzero day,
all of us are trying for compassion.

LAURA MADELINE WISEMAN

South of the Train Tracks

You've been learning how to own a home,
unlearning what you were taught before. Begin
with signing the mortgage for a split-level house
in a blue-collar neighborhood—locksmiths,

electricians, fast-food cashiers, janitors—
all the necessary workers who keep a city
clean, fed, lit with blue light, and open
to whoever might need to get inside.

The job of a new homeowner is to repair,
undo, and upgrade. The original furnace
is the first to go. The stained carpet and pad
pull up easily. The fresh paint smoothes

the walls. Yes, you must call someone
to spray for roaches. Yes, you must save
each month to replace the roof. Yes,
the nearby power lines and factories

give you pause. But the welcome mat
and new bed of roses—all that you do—
lets the young family next door know
you're here to stay and you're one of them.

JOEL PECKHAM

Everything Must Go

In the parking lot, behind the Dollar General, at two
in the afternoon, a young man thrusts hands
into pockets of an old, three-button suit fit
for someone half his size—as if he might
have fished it from a thrift store or a pile
of clothes at a yard sale, estate sale, auction
for the peeling home behind the elementary
school where people pick and peck at tables
on the outgrown lawn, silent as hungry

blackbirds after grubs. Nobody looks
into windows, knocks on doors. Nothing
to see here. Nothing they haven't seen before
on every street in town. Another sign goes
up. Another. And someone gets a tax break
when he buys the place on Market for half
of what it's worth. *And damn, if they'd a let us*
pay that price to start, we could a kept
the bastard. Or if the Ford plant didn't move or if—

And the walls ache empty as the stomachs
of strays who wade sun-splashed in river water
with a girl off Route 222. Everything idles.
Engines low on gas turn, sputter out a grinding
song. Everything's for sale. For rent. Fore
closed. Everything must go. And the young man

hums a melody that could be a spiritual, though
he doesn't look like a boy to sing spirituals. Too
mod, too hip, too fashionably poor. And no one
sings those old songs anymore, having lost the feel,

the touch that looks you up and down and says, *I know,*
because we do. Or should. After all, it's nothing
we haven't heard before: the way we mutter

to ourselves, taking as we do what falls
to us with hands open as any supplicant's. How
many doors swing idly in and out? And tell me who
wore the jackets we are wearing now?

Coming Home

Maggie Boylan got out of treatment at nine in the morning. The third shift monitor was going her way, so he stuck around for the coin ceremony and the speeches and the hugs, and then he took her up to town and dropped her off on the courthouse square. She took a look around, took a deep breath of the open air, and walked straight up to the jailhouse door.

She walked straight back out when they told her that her husband was gone. "We turned him loose a week ago," said Timmy Weatherstone.

She had amends to make to Timmy Weatherstone. She had amends to make to nearly every deputy on the force. And she was ready. But when she heard that Gary had been released, it took her by surprise. Why didn't he call? Why didn't he visit? She blazed a path of curses straight out the door and onto the courthouse lawn. Why hadn't he come to see her like she had come to see him?

After she had cursed Timmy Weatherstone and her husband and her luck from the lawn of the courthouse, she calmed down and thought. She had learned in treatment not to ask so many useless questions; she had learned not to make assumptions. Hell, she thought, Gary's got no license and he's got no car. And nobody's paid the phone bill for thee months.

Edie let her call from the Square Deal Grill and, sure enough, a recording told her that the phone was disconnected.

So she walked to the edge of town and stood on the highway with her thumb out. It was nine miles and a side road to home. It was early spring. The redbuds were out but not yet the dogwoods. There was still some bite in the wind. There were still patches of snowmelt in the shady places along the fencelines and in the ditches. Some girl in treatment had stolen her jacket and her good shoes and left her with these girly thin things that pinched her toes and a little thin jacket that wouldn't hold out the wind. Someone else had left behind a backpack like what a schoolgirl might carry and she had packed it with her Big Book, her clothes, her toothbrush, and other odds and ends. She shivered and stamped, but she was happy to be out on her own and anxious to see Gary again.

It was only a few minutes before a pickup truck pulled over and she thought maybe her luck had begun to turn. It was a big-shouldered, diesel-motored F-150 lugging a stock trailer. She ran down to catch up and the driver opened the door to let her in.

But when she saw who the driver was, she thought, Oh no, this is trouble. It was Joey Ratliff, a boy she knew for all the wrong reasons.

"What's crackin, Maggie?"

"Not much," she said. She hesitated before she climbed up into the cab. He's gonna want me to get him some dope again, she thought. Two hours out of treatment, and I'm already in a risky situation.

"Come on, Maggie," Joey said. "These girls in the trailer aren't too happy with me." The cattle in the trailer were miserable. They moaned and bawled piteously. They pressed their snouts against the slats in the trailer and looked out at Maggie with dark, wet eyes.

"Come on in, and get yourself out of the cold," the boy said.

This won't look good to the judge, Maggie thought. Miller had told her, no contact with known users or dealers or else she would serve the prison time he had suspended. But Miller was not out here standing in the wind with her in a little thin jacket and these little, thin, girly shoes. So she mounted the step into the cab.

Joey Ratliff put the truck into gear and they pulled off with a great rattle of pistons and a mantle of diesel smoke behind them. The boy had the heater cranked up good and warm. The seats were leather and the console was lit up like a small city. Maggie was glad for the warmth, but she tried to keep her head low so no one could see her.

"So what's new, Maggie?"

"Nothin much at all," she told the boy. "I been away."

"I heard," the boy said. "And you just now got out."

"So you heard that too?"

"Word gets around," he said.

"I reckon so."

"You can't cuss out half the sheriff's department on the courthouse square without people knowing Maggie Boylan's back in town."

"Well damn." She fell silent and wanted to think. But it was hard to think with the poor cattle bawling in the trailer. The boy was none too steady on the road and the trailer lurched back and forth across the lanes. The cattle bawled and moaned with every lurch.

"Hell," he said. "it aint nothin."

It was something to Maggie. It could be three years in prison if the judge heard. And how would Miller not hear if this boy had heard already?

"Just party on and forget about it."

"I can't, Joey." Maggie surprised herself by finding the words so easily. "My partyer's broke."

Joey Ratliff pondered this a moment. "That's rough," he said. "I reckon you're just gonna have to accept it. Acceptance," he said, "is the answer to all my problems."

Joey Ratliff had done his time in treatment too.

They were on a downhill curve and the boy had to snatch the wheel hard to the left to keep out of the ditch then to the right to get out of the path of an oncoming car. The trailer behind them rattled over the shoulder gravel and swung into the opposite lane and nearly clipped the car.

Maggie had to grip the door handle to stay in her seat. The cattle, the poor cattle, bawled the louder.

"Damn," Maggie shouted. "You're gonna kill us all."

"It's all right."

She saw, now, that the boy's eyes had an OxyContin glaze on them. His words had an OxyContin loop to them. He drove like someone in an Oxy-Contin haze.

"Joey, you sure you need to be drivin?"

"I'm all right," he said. "Acceptance."

I'm about to accept getting run into one of these telephone poles, Maggie thought. She kept her grip on the door handle and watched the road. Joey wasn't driving fast, but he was nearly always half a beat behind each dip or swerve. Neither spoke for an uncomfortable minute or two. Finally, to make talk, Maggie said, "Your daddy's got a nice truck."

The boy was the son of a county commissioner and things had looked good for him all through high school. College offers, scholarships, all that. But after graduation, he had got caught up in OxyContin, so all his luck and privilege came to nothing. She was not surprised when he asked, "So, Maggie. Can you help me get hold of some Oxy?"

"Can't do it, Joey."

"How about some Vicodin? Percosets?"

"Can't do it."

"Sure you can."

"Does the word *prison* mean anything to you? I got three years settin on the shelf. I'm out of that game altogether."

"Maggie, you know I'm cool."

A truck, passing, barely missed the corner of the stock trailer. "You aint lookin any too cool right now, I'd say."

"Well, if you won't get me some yourself, can you hook me up with those boys on the hill?"

"What boys on what hill?"

"Across the road from your house. Those boys from the city at the old Stephens place."

"Why would I want to do that?"

"You could help a fella out."

"Joey, you're gonna have to help yourself out on this one."

"Come on, Maggie. They don't know me."

"Just ride on up there and get to know em."

"Maggie, you know I can't just do that."

"I don't know what you can and can't do. I just know I can't do that no more."

"Maggie, you never used to be like that."

"I thought you was all about acceptance."

Joey Ratliff geared down to take a hill. "They done something to you in that program. You used to be cool."

"And being cool got me a lot of jail time."

"I can make us some money. I'll pay you."

"I don't need your money. I don't need nothing from you."

"You're gonna need something sometime, cause . . ." He paused.

"Cause what?"

"I probably shouldn't be telling you this . ."

"But you're gonna tell me anyway."

"It's probably none of my business, but . . ."

"You're right, it's none of your business."

"What I'm tryin to say . . ."

"If it's some kind of bullshit, I don't want to hear it."

"How long has Gary been out, Maggie?"

"What difference does it make?"

Joey Ratliff shrugged. "I'm just tryin to tell you something."

"You're tryin to stir up some bullshit is what you're doin."

"I'm just tryin to say . . ."

He did not finish what he was trying to say. They reached the top of the hill at a point where the road curved away to the left. Again, the truck swung right and the trailer with it, and again the boy had to wrench the truck off the shoulder. Again, the trailer swung off the gravel of the shoulder and across both lanes.

"Damn," Maggie said. "You're gonna kill us all for sure." The cattle bawled the louder. "These poor cows are getting beat to death."

"They'll be all right."

"They sure don't think so."

"Those old whores'll be hamburger before the week is out."

Maggie looked back at the trailer, then to the boy. "Joey," she said. "I know you don't have no cattle of your own."

Maggie heard just the slightest hesitation in his voice. "Dad told me, take em to Hillsboro."

"You don't lie good, do you?"

"What're you sayin, Maggie?"

"You don't lie good. If you're gonna lie, do it right."

"Who says I'm lyin?"

"It aint hard to tell. You're stealin your daddy's cattle."

"Maggie, that aint true."

"You owe some money to the boys in town."

"Naw, Maggie."

"Them boys is out to hurt you, so you're gonna sell you daddy's milk cows."

"Maggie . . ."

"But you still want your Oxy, so you want me to hook you up with the boys on the hill cause you aint burnt them yet."

"Oh fuck, Maggie."

"You're a damn thief."

"Look, Maggie, don't be talkin this shit to my dad."

"I got nothing to say to your dad, but I'll say it again to you, you're a fuckin liar and a thief."

The boy shot a look at Maggie. "You've got a lot of nerve talking about me after what you did to Gary."

"What are you talking about?"

"Everybody knows he sat up there in jail for six long months so you wouldn't have to go back to prison."

"Joey, shut up."

"Everybody knows he took the rap for you and now he's got a record and he's lost his job and it's all on account of you."

"Shut up, Joey."

"And while he's settin in jail, you're still doin what you doin til you get a whole new charge."

"Cause some bitch lied on me."

"And Judge Miller thinks he can save your ass, so he gives you treatment instead of prison."

Maggie clenched her jaw and looked straight ahead.

"So you can talk like you got yourself together. You can talk all you want. But I know you're still the same Maggie Boylan."

"You can stop now, Joey."

He would not. "So don't you be talking about me," he said.

Maggie pressed her hands to her ears, but he would not stop.

"Don't be surprised," he said. "Once you get home. You won't find what you think you're gonna find."

He looked her way to emphasize the point. But it was the wrong moment to take his eyes off the road. A rise, a dip, a curve, one after the other and the trailer lashed back and forth across the lanes.

"Oh, my God," Maggie called.

The truck's right front tire tipped over the shoulder and the shoulder was too deep. The steering wheel ripped through the boy's hands to the right and they tilted down into the ditch and mashed to a stop in the buttery mud.

Maggie's seat belt held, but she felt like she had been punched. The cattle bellowed like a grade school band. Maggie glared at the boy but did not yet have the breath to speak.

"Oh, Jesus," the boy said. "I'm screwed."

"I reckon so," Maggie said. Her heart was pounding.

"How are we gonna get out of this?"

"Aint no *we* to it, Joey. I'm gone."

"Wait a minute, you gotta help me get out of this ditch."

"I didn't put you in this ditch, I aint gonna get you out." There was no one out on the road just now, but it would not be long. Someone was sure to hit 911 and here would come the Highway Patrol. Maggie unclipped her seat belt, pulled her backpack from the floor, opened her door and stepped out.

The ditch was half full of runoff and she soaked her feet and the cuffs of her jeans.

"Good luck, Joey," she said. "I got to go."

"You can't leave me like this."

"Just you watch me," she said. "There's nothing I can do to help you and I'm screwed if I stay."

"Maggie, you're a bitch."

"Accept it, motherfucker." She slammed the truck door and climbed out of the ditch.

"I'm gonna call the judge and let him know you was with me."

"Joey, you're gonna do what you're gonna do and I'm gonna do what I'm gonna do." She stepped to the back of the trailer and peered through the slats.

There must have been half a dozen milk cows crowded one on another. The largest of them raised her head and bawled out a long loud lament.

Maggie drew back the slide bolt that held the tailgate closed, opened the gate, pulled out the ramp, and stood back. Not a one of the cows moved. A coffee-eyed calf lowered her head at Maggie and stared.

"Well, cows," she said. "You're on your own from here." She started up the road toward home. At a hundred yards down the road, she looked back. The coffee-eyed calf stood on the shoulder grazing. Joey Ratliff was still in his seat in the cab with his head against the steering wheel. He was either cursing or praying. Maggie could not tell which.

*

The house was cold, but not empty. Gary had taken only what he needed and left the rest to her. He also left a note on the kitchen table.

> *Sorry, Maggie, but enough is enough.*
> *I done all I could and I can't do no more.*
> *I'll be back some time for the table saw,*
> *But I won't stay*

Good luck to you,
Gary

She couldn't blame him. If she had wanted to, she couldn't blame him. They had taken blame away from her in treatment. They had taken her blaming, her lies, her drugs, her thieving, and even her curses. Her curses on the courthouse lawn were her last.

She was as close now to nothing as she had ever been.

She was wet and chilled through and her pinched feet were sore. She found some dry shoes and socks. Gary had left her firewood and she fired up the kitchen stove and the wood stove in the parlor. She fixed herself a plate of food but she could not eat. A familiar, queasy, low-feverish feeling had gripped her at bowel and bone.

But she could not get rid of the chill, no matter how high she stoked the stove. No matter what she did, she could not rid herself of the daunchy feeling in her gut.

Damn, she thought, I come all this way through the program and I'm dope sick all over again.

It did not help that, every hour, cars came back and forth and up and down to the boys on the hill across the road. Somebody was buying and the boys on the hill were selling. All she had to do to get well was cross the road and climb the hill. She wouldn't even need a dime. They would front her, surely, if only so that she would come back later and pay.

The thought brought her relief and terror all in one.

Call somebody, she remembered. But she had no phone. *Go to a meeting,* she remembered. But she had no car. She was stuck in this little farmhouse where every hour, all through the afternoon and into the night, cars from all across the county rumbled over the creek bridge and rattled the gravel of the lane up to the boys on the hill.

The hours ached by. She tried to read her book, but the sickness fuddled her cross-eyed and she could make no sense of the words. She forced herself up off the couch and fretted around the kitchen with her broom and a rag until there was nothing left to clean. She stood, pondering, what do I do now? And how am I gonna get through the night?

From somewhere in the woods or fields nearby, a coyote set up to howl. It sent up a long, lunar lament, made up of sirens and saw blades trailed by a ragged string of yodels and yips. It drew all the dogs up and down the holler out to the ends of their chains to answer back with barks and growls.

But the coyote had said what he had to say. He did not bother to respond. Gradually, the dogs, tired of their argument, crawled one by one back under their porches, and were silent.

That's me all over, Maggie thought. My life's been one long howl. And one big ruckus after another.

Her mind was all atumble. She could not not-think, but to think brought up more thoughts than she wanted to live with.

So fuck it, she thought. Fuck it all.

It would be just a short walk down her lane and across the road, across the narrow bridge over the creek, and up that hill to the house. The lights would be on and the boys would be happy to see her. And of course, they would front her—one or two, or even three or four—enough to get her through this godawful night.

Without willing it or willing against it, she threw the little jacket across her shoulders and stepped into the yard. Without willing it or willing against it, she crossed the yard. At the edge of the road she stopped, out of old habit, and looked to the right and to the left.

Then, when she looked forward again, she saw the coyote in the road. He had not been there when she looked to the right; he had not been there when she looked to the left. But now, as she looked to cross the road, the coyote stood directly in her path. He must have come up from the bed of the creek, she thought. As if in response to the notion, the coyote shook out his coat and cast a silver spray into the moonlight. Maggie stood frozen in place.

The coyote gazed at her, one forepaw raised, as if he were reading her through and through.

Oh my God, she thought, what the fuck am I doing?

She put her hands to her temples and turned back to the house. She stumbled to the couch and collapsed. Shivering, nauseous, utterly emptied of thought, bereft of either hope or despair, she curled up into herself like a child.

Oh my God, she whispered.

As if it were a prayer.

The Last Shot

At sunrise on the Southern Ohio riverbank you can watch spirits dance off the water. Some think the fog is merely there because it's morning, but Keith Sanders went there because he believed it's where the ghosts of men without jobs hovered, trying to figure out how to support their families.

He'd brought a newspaper to sit on so the seat of his pants wouldn't be wet from the morning dew still in the grass. His wife had ironed his periwinkle-blue work shirt the night before, the one that proudly displayed his name in a white rectangle on his chest. His red and white Igloo lunch cooler was full of turkey sandwiches and a love note from his six-year-old daughter Lilly. His tan leather steel-toed boots were worn to the last of their soles. After fifteen years at the bottling factory he was told he was no longer needed. He hadn't had the heart to tell his wife Jill yet, so he set the alarm for its usual time and went to the riverbank to think.

He sat on the riverbank silently, waiting for the sky to lift and reveal citrus shaded clouds. Soon the hills became visible and thousands of trees stood like guards surrounding the water, making sure the prisoners never escaped. His palms pressed to his forehead, he fought to hear his dead father's voice. He wanted an answer as to what he was supposed to do. There were men all over the county that had been waiting for years for something decent and were still pushing a broom and scrubbing toilets on nightshift at local restaurants. The only other option he could think of was to partner up with his friend Jimmy and pray he didn't get caught.

Jimmy had begun a home-grown business. He owned several acres behind his house in McDermott that were mainly hillside and built a dog pen that surrounded his investment. In the hills of Appalachia, dogs were the cheapest home security a man could get. Dogs trained from puppies to protect pot were known to tear off limbs. Jimmy had made more money selling pot in five years than he did at the bottling plant in ten. When people asked how things were going, he would always let his wife Molly have all the credit. "She's workin' down at the Wal-mart now. Who'm I to tell her she can't work? Shit, women get jobs easier than men now, so I say g'on, momma." It always seemed to get a chuckle, but everyone knew Molly's minimum wage job wasn't paying their house payment and keeping their kids in Nike shoes. It's just that no one told, because the majority of people understood it was that or the welfare line. "Keith, when you're ready to trade your old life in for a new one, get yourself a dog, and call me," he'd tell Keith. Keith had never thought about it until now.

Keith hated to think about the predicament his family would be in if he got caught. He couldn't afford to go to jail and have charges permanently on his record; he'd never get hired again once the economy picked back up. But he also couldn't spend one more night watching his wife and daughter suffer through yet another version of Hamburger Helper and Kool-Aid. They didn't mind waiting on payday, but payday wasn't going to come this time.

Keith got up and patted out the wrinkles in his clothes. He folded the newspaper and put it in his back pocket, then picked up his lunch box. With one last glance at the very river that had shipped so many dreams away, he hung his head and begged, *please, someone . . . tell me what to do.*

On his way back up the muddy bank, Keith noticed a woman who had not been on the corner of the bridge before daybreak. The corner of the bridge linking Ohio and Kentucky was the local hotspot for beggars and peddlers. It had more traffic than most of the corners in the city. There was always someone there and the only thing that changed was what they were trying to give away or asking for. The day before yesterday it was a man with a homemade guitar and a veteran jacket singing "Free Bird" and asking for cigarettes. This woman appeared at first to be a beggar holding a sign asking for money. But the closer Keith got, he saw the brown cardboard sign read "FREE PUPPIES" in red marker. The woman wore a faded denim shirt that was easily three sizes too big. She had stringy black and silver hair that floated past her shoulders and next to her feet were three fuzzy brown puppies all tangled up in laundry line rope. The woman smiled at Keith, inviting him to come and look. The dogs were calm and sleeping on the ground between the woman's feet until he began to speak.

"What kind of dogs are these, ma'am?" he asked.

Just as he spoke, one of the puppies woke and began barking and pulling at the line, waking the others.

"I'm afraid they're a mix of just about everything, but they're gonna make good watch dogs. You can't get hardly nothin' past that little fat one right there. We call him Bear." The woman pointed at the dog that had barked at Keith and bent down to pick him up. "He's good with young'uns too, likes to play fetch."

He stared at the dog with deep brown eyes and hesitated making a decision. Regardless of whether he wanted to or not, he had to go home with a way to make things better, he thought.

"All right then. I guess I'll take him home." Keith said.

The woman untied the laundry line from Bear's collar and handed him to Keith.

Keith held the puppy under his right arm, and listened to it grunt every time he took a step. "Damn. Let's hope you don't eat pot, dog. 'Cause it looks like you eat everything else."

Keith put the dog up in the truck seat and called Jimmy. It rang twice before Jimmy picked up.

"What's up, buddy?" Jimmy asked excitedly.

"I got a dog," Keith replied.

The rest of the conversation went just as he assumed it would. Jimmy told him to stop by on the way home. Keith hid the plants in a black garbage bag behind the seat of the truck. He instantly spotted every highway patrolman and deputy on his way home. His temperature would rise and he'd begin to sweat at the thought of an officer pulling up behind him. One sheriff did pull behind him, and the thirty seconds it took to find a driveway to pull off on felt like an hour. His hands shook and he repeatedly peered through the rearview mirror. Bear caught onto the tension and barked loud enough to rattle the windows and turn Keith's eardrums into hollow tunnels. He turned in circles in the seat and jumped up and down. Finally Keith pulled over. The dog kept barking.

"Shut up, dog! Jesus Christ!" Keith yelled, and smacked the dog on its head. He sat in his pickup truck in a stranger's driveway until he could regain composure, taking deep breaths and resting his head on the seat while watching the dog hunker on the floorboard. When an older lady came out the door of the house, he put the truck in reverse and started off again.

Keith pulled into his driveway meeting eyes with his wife who was rocking back and forth on the porch swing of their daisy-colored double-wide trailer. Her eyebrows wrinkled in confusion as to why he was home so early. The small smirk in her perfect rose-shaded lips approved of what she thought was a short work day. Lilly sat on the sidewalk drawing a hop-scotch board with pink chalk and brushing her wild auburn curls from her eyes. She looked up from the sidewalk at the sound of her father's rusted '84 Ford. Excitedly, she tugged at her Little Mermaid nightgown pinned underneath her to let her stand up.

"You're home early, Baby." Jill called out to him, pinning her wet blonde hair to the back of her head. Keith smiled to acknowledge he heard her and walked from the driver's side of the truck to the passenger's and opened the truck door. Bear jumped from the truck into the yard and hiked his leg on Jill's tulips.

"A puppy! Daddy, you got me a puppy! He's so fat!" Lilly screamed in a high soprano squeal. She laughed and ran to Bear.

"Oh no," Jill said in a deep groan. "Where on earth did ya get him?"

"Ha. Well, he was free, and I found him on my way home."

"So Lilly wore you down, I guess. What happened to the firm stand we were taking on the *No Dogs Allowed* rule?" Jill asked. She wrapped her arms around Keith's waist and put her hands in his back pockets. "I missed you this morning," she added while lightly kissing his cheek.

Keith kissed her forehead and rested his face in her hair, breathing the apple-scented shampoo. He held her to his chest, knowing she'd be upset once he started talking.

"I gotta tell ya some things, starting with why there's a dog." Keith whispered.

Jill pulled back from him and looked into his dark blue eyes. "Sounds serious."

"It is. Let's go inside." He patted her shoulders and pulled away. "Let's get the dog, and I have somethin' else I gotta get out of the truck."

"Lilly? Lilly? Where'd ya go baby?" Jill questioned. Her eyes scanned the yard.

"I'm in here, Mommy," Lilly giggled. She scuffed through the bushes holding Bear with both hands and struggled to keep hold while he wiggled and yapped.

"Let's go inside and find him a blanket. Mommy and Daddy need to talk."

Lilly headed up the sidewalk toting the dog and passing the sidewalk chalk on her way. Jill walked behind her, occasionally looking back at Keith struggling to pull a black garbage bag from the back of the truck seat. Keith broke it loose and walked the sidewalk to the door with his new investment.

His initial conversation starter of *I lost my job but I'm gonna grow pot with Jimmy* didn't go over well. It was followed quickly by *You don't even know how to grow pot! You smoked it what, once in high school?* Knowing it was going to be a long night, Keith sat at the kitchen table they had prayed at over many meals.

"It's not that you lost your job and didn't tell me, it's that you brought home drugs." Jill screamed, while Lilly laid on the couch upside down, the dog jumping from the floor into her hair.

"What is it that you want me to do, Jill? What choices do I have?"

"We'd find somethin'. I can work. Jimmy's wife works."

"It's not that I don't want you to work, it's that it won't be enough. My job brought home what three minimum wage jobs brought, Jill. There is nothing else."

Jill lifted her hands and buried her face in them, trying not to cry.

"You tell me what to do and I'll do it. This is the only thing I know to do. I need to be able to take care of my own, Jill. It's what I was taught to do."

Jill uncovered her eyes, and stared back into the living room where Lilly had let out a scream. Bear was pulling backward with a mouthful of Lilly's hair in a tug of war with her scalp.

"Let go, Bear! Mommy! It's eating me!" Lilly cried.

"I'll tell ya what to do, Keith," she yelled, and pointed into the living room. "Go get the damn piss bag that's devouring your daughter and make it a bed outside, and you might wanna think about making you one out there, too."

Keith slept in the camper parked beside the garage for two nights. He had nowhere to be and nothing to do but think. Jill barely spoke to him but to pass the phone to him when someone had called to say they were sorry to hear the news about the plant going under. Each offered condolences, but no jobs, no real ideas. With each phone call he became more embarrassed that the only thing he'd accomplished was emptying a case of beer and a bottle of bourbon, and chucking the bottles side by side next to the fire-pit, letting them clink off one another. Lilly had brought him sandwiches around lunchtime each day and said *Thanks for taking care of my dog, Daddy.* He wanted to tell her that he was just trying to take care of her, too, but Jill hurried her to come back inside. Keith knew Jill hated when he drank because he spoke his mind without thinking. It's why he didn't do either often. Words were hard to take back, but that didn't mean he never tried.

On the third evening it was cold. He sat slumped in a metal lawn chair with a baseball cap lowered over bloodshot eyes and stared at the dog he'd tied up. With every hour that passed, he regretted bringing it home. He'd pulled an empty garbage can up to a tree and buried his daughter's old *Care Bears* comforter in the back of it for the dog to sleep on. The dog had a better bed than he did. It pulled at the line and barked to be loose, yelping and whining, ungrateful for what he'd tried to do for it. Bear was at the worst he'd been for days. He would occasionally stop barking long enough to lap up a drink of water and cough, then start again.

"Shut up, dog! Please, just shut the hell up," he shouted.

The dog barked back.

"Shut up! Jesus Christ! We don't even want ya now."

Yet again, the dog barked and begged.

"What the hell's going on out there?" Jill called out. She poked her head halfway out the screen door.

"Nothin'. Go back in the house where you belong," Keith replied, rising from his chair to face her.

"What did you just say to me?" Jill asked. She stepped out the door onto the porch, and crossed her arms in front of her.

"I said, go back in the house where you belong! That's your job, this is mine. Remember? You made that clear several days ago."

"Oh, really?" Jill took a step forward. Keith stepped closer to her, trying to intimidate her back inside. He beat the ground as he walked and she stood firm until he reached the bottom step of the porch. Jumping three steps to land on the top one, he gained footing and grabbed the handle of the screen door. Jill tried to hold it shut from the inside.

"Open the damn door, Jill!" Keith yanked and pulled on the door, causing Jill to lose her footing on the other side. The door swung open and Keith stepped over her to get in.

"This is my house too, and if I wanna come in, I'll come in!"

Jill sat on the linoleum and listened to the dog barking outside. She pulled herself up and pushed Keith out of her way. "What are you gonna do with the fuckin' pot, Keith?" Jill asked.

"I don't want it in this house. I don't want people comin' here to buy it and

I don't want people comin' here to steal it. And I don't want you in here drunk and scary. You are not this man. We have a six-year-old daughter for God's sake."

Keith was beginning to feel the heat in his face and the strain in his eyes. His hands shook. He noticed Lilly out of the corner of his eye run with a flashlight and cheese crackers. His heart sank at the thought that they were scared of him.

"I won't let anyone hurt you, Jill."

"Really, Keith? How are you gonna do that, when the damned dog doesn't even know what to bark at? The thing is gonna keep us up all night barking at mosquitoes! And if you get caught, you know what that means? It means I'm raisin' Lilly by myself," she said, while counting reasons on her fingers. "We're gonna lose the house and not have anywhere to live, and you're gonna be in jail and not able to get another job, 'cause you'll be a criminal," she added, throwing her hands in the air. "This is the way it starts, Keith. People think they can just sell pot until they see what kind of money comes in with pills. Then the shit just keeps escalatin' until it's out of control." He refused to make eye contact. Voice cracking, she decided to give the final shove. "Your Daddy would be ashamed!"

Keith gritted his teeth and pointed his finger at her, growling at her low blow. He knew she was right, but it felt like gasoline had been poured on the last ounce of integrity he had left and set ablaze. "Fine, you want me to take it all back, that's fine. I can do that. I've done it before." He grabbed the black garbage bag from beside the couch and his shotgun from behind the door.

"What are you doing, Keith? Keith!" Jill screamed as she tugged at his wrist to hold him back. The dog barked louder, competing with their screaming, and she knew what the shotgun was for.

He ran down the steps of the porch and threw the bag beside the firepit. His flannel shirt, loose at the sides and dangling, framed his arms as he cocked his shoulders up to see through the aim of his gun. The dog stood facing Keith at the entry of the garbage can, and, although its mouth was opening and closing, there was no sound, as if Keith were deaf to the world's complaints around him. He squeezed the trigger and saw the smoke of the slug leaving the barrel at the same time he saw a light flicker in the garbage can, and little fingers emerge from behind the *Care Bears* blanket.

DAVID BAKER

Patriotics

Yesterday a little girl got slapped to death by her daddy,
    out of work, alcoholic, and estranged two towns down river.
America, it's hard to get your attention politely.
    America, the beautiful night is about to blow up

and the cop who brought the man down with a shot to the chops
    is shaking hands, dribbling chaw across his sweaty shirt,
and pointing to cars across the courthouse grass to park.
    It's the Big One one more time, July the 4th,

our country's perfect holiday, so direct a metaphor for war
    we shoot off bombs, launch rockets from Drano cans,
spray the streets and neighbors' yards with the machine-gun crack
    of fireworks, with rebel yells and beer. In short, we celebrate.

It's hard to believe. But so help the soul of Thomas Paine,
    the entire country must be here—the acned faces of neglect,
the halter-tops and ties, the bellies, badges, beehives
    jacked-up cowboy boots, yes, the back-up singers of democracy

all gathered to brighten in unambiguous delight
    when we attack the calm pointless sky. With terrifying vigor
the whistle-stop across the river will lob its smaller arsenal
    halfway back again. Some may be moved to tears.

We'll clean up fast, drive home slow, and tomorrow
    get back to work, those of us with jobs, convicting the others
in the back rooms of our courts and malls—yet what
    will be left of that one poor child, veteran of no war

but her family's own? The comfort of a welfare plot,
    a stalk of wilting prayers? Our fathers' dreams come true as nightmare.

So the first bomb blasts and echoes through the streets and shrubs:
    red, white, and blue sparks shower down, a plague

of patriotic bugs. Our thousand eyeballs burn aglow like punks.
    America, I'd swear I don't believe in you, but here I am,
and here you are, and here we stand again, agape.

Destroying New Boston

There was no reason for us to believe there would be diesel in the tank. We'd watched that mill decay since childhood, heard unemployed and underemployed fathers throw back six-packs and curse its existence. Why would the crane have still had juice?

It seemed comical to watch Edith scamper up the substructure of the crane and do her goofy little dance at the top. But being Edith, she had to take things a step too far, and then it all went down. She hopped into the cab and gleefully jabbed at buttons, pulled levers, kicked at the foot pedals. She sat down in the operator's stool and waved down to us, princess-style. That's when Jake noticed it.

"Did you guys hear something?"

We did—the rumble of an engine, followed shortly by a godawful guttural groaning. The sound of gears turning.

I flailed my arms in warning, but she couldn't see a thing. Sam and Jake screamed at me to stop when I launched myself up the ladder, leapt into the cab where Edith was frozen in place, her eyes open wide and her skin somehow even paler than normal—even her freckles seemed to have gone white. That's when I did what any teenaged would-be hero must: I slammed every button I could find, including the big red joystick in the middle. In hindsight, that's one I should've avoided. But somewhere in the frenzy of my motion, I whacked it, jarred it to the right. It stuck. The hulking machine turned clockwise, slowly at first, but by the end of the first revolution it was already moving at a good clip.

Edith unfroze long enough to say, "Jump?"

We grabbed each other's hand and did just that. We cleared the cab, tumbled onto the platform, and then hurried down a rusty ladder to the ground. The cab spun in faster circles. The crane arm, its cable, and the attached hook became a giant whip—a wrecking ball spinning in great broad circles, cartoon-like. It hit a small coal shed first—that ramshackle job of rebar and corrugated steel sheets stood no chance. The hook broadsided the main coke oven and must've struck dead on a main beam, because that building, the most recognizable piece of our miserable little city, trembled for about ten seconds, and then collapsed on itself. I followed my friends toward the street, not yet feeling the cuts, scrapes and bruises I'd gathered in my fall. Behind our backs, we heard a crash—a small section of the conveyor lines crashing into the Ohio.

When we reached the abandoned Norfolk-Southern yard, we all stood there breathless, terrified, accidentally triumphant. Jake wore the biggest grin I'd ever seen on him, and Sam just stared blankly. Though I never saw him with a joint, I suspect that Sam was either perpetually stoned or deeply frayed, emotionally. In that moment, though, he was blank with *awe*. Edith and I looked at each other, wide-eyed, then surveyed our handiwork as we tried to capture our breath.

"Dude," Jake said. "You two just destroyed New Boston."

Of course, we hadn't—we'd just destroyed the part of New Boston that had destroyed the rest of New Boston. But that was good enough. Much better than our normal Tuesday routine, which involved splitting a six-pack of generic soda and chucking rocks from the bluff-top high school parking lot.

We would later swear that we presided over our triumph until the first of the plant's massive smokestacks tipped over and came hurtling directly at us. In reality, it was the sound of approaching sirens that prompted retreat. Running, I thought of my father's face the night he came home and sat down as if nothing had happened. His eyes were so blank and empty that night, his face pale and expressionless. He shut the blinds, then slumped all night on the sofa and stared at the black television screen—he never used to shut those blinds, so I knew something was bad wrong. Later that night when I snuck out of bed and peeked through them, I saw, for the first time, what the nighttime skyline looked like without a pilot light blazing. He never looked the same to me after that night. The color never fully returned to his face, the life never completely returned to his eyes. So as I hurdled pieces of wreckage and fled the scene, I smiled for him. I smiled for all the fathers and families whose trajectories were mutilated by that place. I imagined that if Dad had known this would be so easy, he'd have swigged a longneck or five and climbed into that crane himself, years earlier.

*

We thought it was over—we didn't expect the aftershock. It must've been the sudden resumption of motion at the long-dormant site, all that stored-up energy hidden down in the sooty dirt, and we'd set it loose. We reached the top of the hill, our normal roost, just in time to see that first stack fall, right across the rail lines where we'd stood ten minutes earlier. Edith's eyes got all wide, and Sam gave Jake a big oh, hell look.

A few seconds later, as if waiting for the cue of our full attention, the easternmost stack crumbled. The center stack, the tallest one, wavered for a few seconds, like a great middle finger, flipping one last bird at the town before it collapsed on itself.

"Shit, dude," Sam said, his tone even-keeled and bored as ever. "Shit." Jake faced Edith, grabbed her by the belt, pulled her against him, wrapped his arm around her back and kissed her. After a few seconds of frantic slurping, Jake let her go, staggered backward, said, "You are a god."

*

A couple hours later, we were screwing around in the Dollar General, avoiding our homes—we looked fine to each other but knew our parents would take one look at us see guilt written in the boldest letters.

"They're looking for you, you know." The clerk—I couldn't remember her name, she'd quit coming to school earlier in the year—said this very matter-of-factly.

"For what?" Jake asked.

The clerk just laughed at him.

He stepped forward and placed his hands on the counter as if he was going to intimidate her. "How the hell do they *know?*"

She pointed at the police scanner, turned on low behind the counter.

"Somebody saw you running, told the cops," the girl said, then she smiled. "Take some gum on your way out. On me."

I grabbed a pack of Winterfresh, but put it back when no one else took any.

Around the corner at Wippy Dip, the manager leaned through the service window and gave us a thumbs-up.

"How the hell do these people even know who we are?" I whispered to Edith.

"I don't know," she said. "Maybe it'd help if you didn't look so guilty. Stop looking guilty." I guess she could tell it was striking me right then that we were about to be in it deep over what we'd done, so she playfully smacked my shoulder to take the edge off her remark. It didn't work.

Meanwhile, Jake was stalking up to the window like he does when he's pissed. He looked like he was about to deck the poor burger guy, and so we stopped to see what would happen. Jake leaned forward, and what we wouldn't have given to hear what he said then, but when he turned around a minute later, he had an armful of burgers and fries. "Our reward," he said, and we took over a picnic table.

"What about drinks?" Sam asked.

"That's just greedy," Jake said. "Shut up and eat your fries."

I didn't understand how they could just sit and eat like that, out in public, in the middle of everything. We were wanted—people were out there searching for us, and someone already taken the liberty of ratting us out. I managed about five bites of food; while they joked around and told stories about gym class, I focused most of my energy on repressing vomit.

*

Later on, Jake told us to follow him, which kind of went without saying. We followed him most of the time as it was, but we were particularly okay with following in this instance, since he was the only one with experience running from anything. We hung back for a moment when he strolled through the door of the Brass Pony Club. A second later, he stuck his head out the door and waved us in. None of us was eighteen, and we were all broke. It took about five minutes for us to realize that a strip club was a really dumb place to be with empty pockets and a preexisting guilt complex, so we filed right back out. Still, we'd been inside, and we were pretty certain that would carry some nice lunchroom cred. On the way out, a manager with a lopsided goatee shook our hands, congratulated us and said, "Make sure y'all come see us again when you get out."

Sam flipped him off, and the bouncer chuckled, but we still walked a little faster, watched behind us for flashing lights. Once we'd cleared the block, Jake pointed toward the river. "Bridge?" he asked.

"Bridge," Sam confirmed, and we made for the riverfront, scaled the overland tresswork of the L&N Railroad Bridge. Despite red-lettered *Beware* signs posted everywhere, it was perfectly safe to climb. It was more or less abandoned. The coal trains coming up from Kentucky had gotten so long and so heavy they had to cross the gleaming new reinforced bridge east of Huntington—New Boston wasn't even a viable shortcut anymore.

Jake reached back to help Edith up, but she climbed onto the deck herself, scrambling with a hilarious, frantic leg kick. Even through the deck was solid, we balanced on the rails—it just seemed the right way to cross. We stopped midway and sat, dangled legs out over the river. We gazed back at town, at the new skyline we'd created.

"Looks even more dead," Sam said.

"Just looks honest," Jake said.

The front tip of a downbound barge crept under the bridge, empty—its great open bins waiting for their next load of coal or ore. Sam searched the deck for a suitable rock, then launched a golf ball-sized hunk of limestone at the barge. For a good ten seconds, it danced and pinged around the hopper. A crewman ran out of the pilothouse, to investigate the sound, to determine whether it was the bridge falling apart, or the barge. Sam whistled and waved at the man, who aimed his light at us and then waved back. We saw the quick flick of a lighter and then the glowing pinprick that every few seconds swung an arc between his hip and his lips, until the barge started its swing around the bend and he dropped his cig, ran into the cabin to fetch the rest of the crew. A few seconds later, his silhouette reemerged, pointing out the newly flat riverfront.

The bridge was the only point from which New Boston had ever really looked like a city, and only at night when the functionless shells of buildings stood in for all the nothingness that was *really* there. For the first time that night, we got to see our town for what we knew it to be. Behind us, to the east, twin halos of light that marked Ashland and Huntington were reassuring reminders that there are places that don't mind being lit, that don't mind being seen.

"You see that?" Edith asked.

She pointed toward the bank. Through the gaps where infrastructure once stood, a couple flashlight beams bounced off windows and guardrails near the plant entrance.

"That's for us?" Jake asked.

I nodded. "Imagine so."

Sam grinned a little sheepishly.

"We're celebrities," Jake said.

I shook my head. "No. They're just bored. What else does anyone have to do on a Tuesday?"

"Either way," Sam said, "they're going to catch us."

"No shit," Jake said. "But it's worth it, right?"

Nobody answered him—we all just sat there and stared at our handiwork. I looked at Sam on my right, at Jake and Edith on my left, and imagined this moment was the pinnacle for us, that we would look back on that point in much the same way our classmates might remember a particular high school football game, or being crowned homecoming queen, or having their first intentional kid. *As good as it gets.* I knew Sam and Jake and Edith had no particular plans to leave town, and even though I assumed I'd eventually move on, it seemed in that moment highly unlikely that any event in my life could ever top that night. And for the moment, that was okay—as far as seminal moments go, I could've done worse. I decided it would make for the sort of story that would someday cause my kids to grimace while I told my grandkids about it in brutal, exaggerated detail. Nothing against the traditional pinnacles of highschoolness, but ours was much cooler than playing a game in tight pants or spending a couple of hours in a plastic crown.

Sam chucked one last rock into the river, and we watched the resulting rings spread out and diffuse, then stood in wordless unison, balanced the rail back to shore, and started toward the residential district.

*

When we turned the corner onto Sycamore, a cop car waited in Jake's driveway—his dad leaned on the cruiser, smoking and having a laugh with the men who sought his son. The familiar anger vein jutted out from the side of Jake's neck, and I grabbed onto his wrist, pulled him backward. It wasn't going to do us any good if he socked his old man, right in front of a cop. We made for the apartment complex where Edith's mother lived, but a city cop was smoking in the stairwell. By this point, lights were making us jumpy so we headed for Sam's through dimmer alleys. A sheriff leaned on his cruiser, which was parked sideways, blocking the driveway as if we were going to run the blockade in our nonexistent cars. My place was farthest away, and the unspoken hope was that no one had bothered to check there. They must've been out of police cars, because, honest to God, a fire truck sat in the driveway. Mom and Dad stood on the porch with arms folded.

Mom was clearly crying. Dad had his arm wrapped around her, and he looked furious. I hadn't really wanted to go home—we were following Jake fairly blindly by that point—and that sight reinforced my instinct.

Of all the people who could've spotted us, it was one of the firemen who shouted and pointed as we ducked below the fence line. We bolted, still hunched over so they wouldn't see our heads over the fence. For a moment, we tried to keep up with Jake, but he had too much experience with this sort of thing and made for a stand of trees; we couldn't keep up. When he turned and briefly paused to wait for us, Edith was the only one who made the effort to continue. Sam just shook his head and walked back toward downtown. I shrugged and stayed put. "Suit yourselves," Jake said. "Good luck."

I waited for a moment, watched them make their getaways toward hiding places amongst empty buildings and burnt-out streetlights. I suppose theirs was the logical choice, but I wasn't going to waste that night hiding. I went back to the mill.

*

I felt like it should be hard work getting there, and so I slipped along the brick wall of an abandoned upholstery shop, then got cute and decided to scale a fence with action-flick speed. Good thing Dad insisted on buying us cheap jeans: I'd have been stuck hanging upside-down if they hadn't torn so damn easily. As it turned out, I was suspended just an instant—not even long enough to extend my arms and buffer the impact—before I plunged squarely on my head. The resulting bump, along with some mild blackening of the left eye, looked completely badass in my mug shot. It hurt less than the realization, when I stood and looked around, that absolutely no one was following me.

I used a bit more care when I hopped the limp barbed wire and re-entered the crime scene. I picked up the first blunt object that didn't seem likely to tear open my palms, scaled the nearest pile of rubble. I was done keeping quiet and holding back. When I lifted that slim stripe of heavy-gauge pipe over my head ready for that first strike, I felt more powerful than I'd managed to in seventeen previous years, probably combined. As I set my shoulder muscles into motion and sent the hollow rod screaming downward, I thought of everything else that could have possibly destroyed this place—a swollen Ohio, an explosive mishap, an earth-scorching blast at the uranium enrichment plant a few miles inland or downstream at the nuclear power station. But we had done it. We had taken down the mill, and I wanted to kick it while it was down.

The pipe was crummy as a destructive tool, but even the smallest crack in a piece of concrete, or the divorce of a few long-mortared bricks felt cathartic. When I struck, the pipe pinged and then reverberated the way my Little League bat had the day I forgot to pack batting gloves for practice. This time, I didn't complain. It was painful and clunky, but still gave more satisfaction than my truest of hits the day Dad handed me a nine iron at the driving range.

"World's best way to blow off stress," he had said, then clobbered a shot off the 150-yard sign. Until the night at the mill, I believed him.

It was divine providence—maybe willed into being by Dad, I thought— when I found a real, honest-to-God sledgehammer resting right out in open space, rusted, halfway sunk in a patch of mud, and practically begging to be used again. When I made my first solid contact with that monster— God, it felt amazing, as if the world slowed as I swung so that I could feel each vein pulse and each muscle fire in a quickening chain from my legs to hips, then through my back and shoulders and arms until the hammer struck concrete and all my force and momentum stopped and my whole body shook, my fingers trembled and I saw the crumbled piece of mess I'd made out of something once solid. It seemed as if the sledgehammer had been invented for just such a moment, as if I were the lone person who would ever feel the instrument's proper use. I took my new implement to the highest point of the tallest rubble pile I could find, and started bashing it down from the top. It was up there that I first had the sensation of not being alone. All the way on the other side of the mess we'd made, down by the barge dock, I swore I heard another sound, another rhythmic clink. I imagined another figure lifting, dropping, destroying, hoisting.

I moved toward the sound and thought that maybe it was a cop, or maybe one of the others, Jake or Sam or Edith, struck with the same idea. Then it occurred to me that it could be my father, a solitary form hammering away, helping put the death knell to this place. I stopped and smiled at this idea, imagined his taut back and broad shoulders covered in flannel, hoisting the red-handled pick axe that most nights rested on a hook above the garage workbench. I imagined how he'd look as I stepped up and joined him, stood at his side. He would give me a goofy, kidlike grin, like the ones he used to wear before *that night*—and put his arm around my shoulder.

"You wrecked this place," he would say, and then we would stand and destroy together, take out our aggression on that hollow place.

But of course, when I got there, the sound was just the clinking of a piece of chain against a flagpole, jostled rhythmically by the wind. I surveyed the ground for a moment, disappointed my daydream had been just that. Dad was sitting at home, pissed off and waiting for me to sneak in the back door or to be led through the front in cuffs. He was comforting Mom, and marinating the months' worth of icy glares and angry remarks that were coming my way.

I took aim at the nearest building and leveled the hammer, swung it until my arms were too spent to lift once more. Even then, I tried again and got it only a foot off the ground before the whole thing, handle and all, plunked harmlessly next to my sneaker. I never felt the pain until I stopped, but in that instant when I resolved my work was done, each finger, both palms throbbed and ached with brutal force. Brick dust and concrete dust, and plain old dirt dust were caked onto the film of blood that had apparently coated my hands. My ribs, my back, my legs, my head—everything throbbed and ached. The tips of my fingers tingled and would not stop; as much as I hated that feeling, I focused on it because in that moment, it was the least awful sensation I felt.

I wanted to keep the hammer with me as a sort of memento, but knew wherever I was headed when morning came, I wouldn't be allowed to bring it along. So I left it where it lay and once more scaled the fence. This time, each link tore into broken, grime- and blood-encrusted hands—but it was worthwhile excruciation. I left the mill grounds, crossed the street, and climbed the crumbling stairway up to the high school parking lot. The football stadium was unlocked, and so I let myself in, climbed the bleacher steps two at a time, and scaled the press box.

I looked out at the dark field before me. This is where Dad had taken me the day after the plant closed. Longing for redemption or hope, a record crowd showed up to watch Wheelersburg run the score to 56–3 before their coach finally sent in his scrubs with three minutes left. Everyone stayed, though, glued to their spots through the whole bludgeoning, as if looking for hope right up until the end. Perched at our regular spot, bleacher seats

18 and 19 in Row G overlooking the 40-yard-line, I sat next to my father and watched him weep like a baby. He tried like hell to kill those tears, wiping them away with a flannel sleeve. But the sleeve was still full of fly ash from the mill, and it just irritated his eyes and increased the general wetness of the moment. I sat there and watched the slump-shouldered footballers sulking to the locker room. I tried to stare at girls in cheer skirts, at newspapermen popping off shots as fast as they could wind their film. Finally, I gave up the distractions and put my arm around Dad. It was the only time I ever saw him cry. And it was the saddest thing I've ever seen.

The night we took down the mill, I sat up there alone with those sad images bouncing around in my head and I waited for someone to come after me, watched for motion down below. I looked for signs that anyone cared. I fell asleep waiting.

The Jesus Lights

Farrell Johnson never had much in this world except a wife and a son and six rocky acres that his granddad left him. When he was nineteen, he ruined his back helping Clarence Myers pull a dead calf out of one of his heifers. They let him go at the sawmill over that. The doctor said he'd never work again, but once Farrell could gimp around a little, Clarence talked one of his trustee buddies into getting him on with the township road crew. That was back in 1968, not long after he and Cindy got married, and he's been with them ever since. The township can't afford to work him more than a couple days a week, but they allow him to stay on the good insurance. Sometimes he flags the traffic; sometimes he drives the truck. Most days he still wears a truss.

Farrell's son, Charley, got himself killed a long time ago in a fast car over on Storm Station Road. He was the third boy from Knockemstiff to flip over the bank at the S curves in less than a year. Whenever Farrell thought about that night, he tried to picture one in which Charley touched the brakes just right, slid out of the bend with maybe his heart up in his throat, but still pumping blood through his veins. The way he imagined it, the boy would have come home after burning up all his gas, and Farrell would have gotten a chance to tell him he was sorry about their fight. For sure, Cindy would have left him—the only thing she was waiting on by then was Charley's high school graduation—but Farrell figured he could have survived that. After the back injury, he'd never had any business being with a woman anyway, especially not one with pants as hot as Cindy's. And though it's true that Charley might have always considered him a coward, Farrell would have been more than happy to live with that, too.

But Charley didn't keep the car on the road; and Cindy never left. Instead, they found what was left of the boy's heart stuck to the end of the steering column; and she went back to the trailer right after the funeral and cut up all her pretty dresses into rags except for one. Even as sick as he felt over his son, Farrell couldn't help but get his hopes up a little, thought that maybe she was getting ready to be a wife again. He was still waiting on that to happen when she came in the kitchen a few days later, told him to bring Charley's Mustang home. He tried to talk her out of it, but she jabbed her cigarette in his coffee cup and called the wrecker man herself. "Look, it's gonna be hard enough as it is," Farrell said after she got off the phone. "Why would we want to look at that thing?"

Rather than answer him, Cindy took another Pall Mall from her housecoat and lit it at the stove. As Farrell watched her walk back into the living room, he realized that making things right between them hadn't even crossed her mind. That afternoon, she had the wrecker man set the smashed-up Ford down in the front yard under the big sycamore that Charley used to swing on when he was a kid. The man hopped down off his tow truck with his hat in his hands and offered to buy the fancy hubcaps for his own son's car, but Cindy wouldn't hear of it. Then a couple nights later, someone stole them. Two sets of footprints in the snow led Farrell over the hill to Jim Pritchard's house. He stood at the fence line for a few minutes, watching gray smoke rise from Jim's chimney and wishing he was out patching potholes on the road. He recalled a preacher telling his granddad one time when the old man was going through one of his bad times, "Alvin, hanging onto the dead don't do you any good." But Charley had baled hay and picked apples for four years to buy that car, and Farrell finally went on up to the house. Nobody answered when he knocked on the door. Walking out to the pole barn, he found the wheel covers hid under a piece of brown felt. When he got back home, he nailed them to a wall in the shed. They've been there ever since.

Months went by when Cindy didn't say two words to Farrell. They grew old watching the weather fade the Mustang's blue paint to gray, the bloodstains to white splotches. He planted flowers around it every spring—marigolds and hollyhocks and Johnny jump-ups—and it didn't look quite so sad and rusted out with some bright blooms standing up against it. They kept Charley's room just like he left it, with the star map taped to the ceiling above the bed and the pillow flopped on the floor. Each evening, Cindy set a place for him at the table. She always buttered him a heel of bread, which was what he liked most. She stared at his plate all the time she was eating, waiting for his ghost to start gnawing on something, while Farrell sat across from her and hoped that never happened.

Other than grieving over the boy, the only thing that Cindy did was watch the talk shows on TV. Farrell didn't mind that she left everything up to him; if nothing else, he figured that taking care of her and the trailer was probably what had kept him going all these years. He'd learned a long time ago that staying busy is the best way to get by in this world; and he would have rather cleaned out ditches along the road with a teaspoon than listen to some blubbering woman confess on the *Lance Willoughby Show* to having dirty thoughts about her husband's own sister. The way Farrell saw it, the Lord only gives you so much time, and to waste it on such stupidity is just as much a sin as most.

Every summer, he raised a big garden across the creek, and he spent a lot of time over there, just sitting and watching things grow. He had an old lawn chair under an apple tree that his granddad had planted soon after returning from the First World War. If Farrell looked hard enough, he could still see the old man's initials carved into the bark right above his own. His family had been on this piece of ground for over a hundred years, and he hated to think what would happen to it after he was gone. It was bad enough tearing the old house down when Cindy wanted to buy the trailer, but ever since Charley died, he'd had to face the fact that someday a stranger would move in and wipe away any sign that a family named Johnson had ever lived here at all.

As far as he could tell, Cindy never shut the TV off. Sometimes he took a sleeping bag over to the garden rather than listen to it cackle all night. There was a spot beyond the beans that he kept planted thick in clover, and it was soft as any bed. Once he got stretched out, he tried to study the stars some, like he used to do with Charley. He could remember when he and the boy used to stay up half the night with a flashlight and an almanac, tracking the constellations and learning the names of stars. Farrell's granddad had done the same with him, pointing out the outlines of Cepheus and Pisces and Gemini with the chewed-up stem of his pipe. The old man had come back from France a twitchy, red-eyed insomniac, and he spent years memorizing the Heavens while everyone else was in bed. "When I was over there in them trenches," he told Farrell a hundred times, "the only thing that kept me believing in God was the sky on a clear night. You'd be stuck knee-deep in that stinking mud, and it seemed like the whole world was turning to shit." Those had been the best times of Farrell's life, the hours he spent looking at the glittering black sky with his granddad and then Charley. But now, sixty-two years old and worn to a frazzle, the sound of the water trickling by in the creek put him to sleep faster than anything, and most mornings he couldn't even recall if he'd seen the Scorpion or not.

On the twenty-first anniversary of Charley's death, Farrell got up early and put the finishing touches on his wreath. The boy had the wreck just a week shy of Christmas, and every year on that day he and Cindy drove over to the cemetery to decorate the grave. Once he was done preparing the wreath, Farrell cleaned up the mess, tossed the leftover pieces of evergreen and grape vine out the back door, put away the snips and the little roll of wire. He was on his fourth cup of coffee when he heard Cindy get up and start moving around. Except to see the doctor, the only time she ever left the trailer was the day they went to the cemetery. She always got dressed up, wore the one dress she'd saved back from the day of the funeral, a pair of scuffed high heels she kept in a box under her bed.

What once took her an hour now took all day, and Farrell decided he needed to kill some time. Around noon, he washed out his cup and walked down the holler to the store. He spent the next several hours sipping on a bottle of Seven-Up and listening to Hank go on about the Reds. The storekeeper had been working at Maude's even longer than Farrell had been with the township. Every time he got a little alcohol in him, he'd start in about driving down to Cincinnati to take in a double-header. "By God, I'm going next year no matter what," he said that afternoon. "I might even get me one of those hotel rooms and stay the night." Usually, Farrell didn't pay much attention to his friend's worn-out pledges, but today they reminded him of all the times he'd told Charley he was going to buy a telescope. When Hank bent down and reached into the meat case for another Old Milwaukee, Farrell slipped out the door and headed back up to the trailer.

He found Cindy on the couch, taking the pink rollers out of her thinning gray hair. Her hands shook a little, and a new tic he hadn't noticed before kept pulling at her left eye. Sitting down in a chair across from her, he glanced out the window toward the Mustang in the yard. He could see his wife's pale, wavering reflection in the glass; and it occurred to him that she was now just as much a ghost as the one she buttered the bread for every night at the dinner table. "It's gonna be dark by the time we get there," he finally said.

She looked up at him, then out the window. Long black shadows stretched across the gravel road out front. Dropping the last roller in a paper sack, she reached for a tube of lipstick on the coffee table. The old dress hadn't fit quite right for several years; but when Cindy stood and walked across the room to look in the mirror hanging on the wall, it slid completely off her shoulders, revealing a loose bra stained yellow with age. "Give me fifteen minutes," she told Farrell, pulling the dress back up. "And would you mind finding somewhere else to sit? You're making me nervous."

He carried the wreath out to the van and started the engine, checked the air in the tires and wiped off the windshield. By the time they started for the cemetery, it was nearly five o'clock. The pale sun was already skimming the tops of the trees over on the Mitchell Flats. On the corner across from the store was Wilma Watson's house, and there she was out in the yard with her son, Tom, and his two little girls. They were helping Wilma put up the wooden Jesus, the one her husband made right after he got saved and right before the cancer took him. Farrell had been at the church the night that Bill got up and testified. Though they hadn't spoken in years, he'd helped the sick man back to his seat when his legs gave out from under him at the altar. A few days later, Bill pulled up beside him in his pickup as Farrell was walking down to the store. "I'm headed for the lumber yard," Bill said. "Gonna build me a Jesus."

"That right?"

"Yeah," Bill said. He handed Farrell a picture out the truck window of the Savior that he'd torn out of an old *Watchtower* magazine. "You figure that's a true likeness of him? I'd ask the preacher, but all he wants to talk to me about is the afterlife."

Farrell glanced down at the picture, thought about telling Bill that he'd read in a book once that the Savior probably had dark skin and a black beard. He also considered just telling Bill to go fuck himself, something he should have done years ago. But when he looked at his neighbor and saw the deep grooves that sickness had dug into his splotchy face, the purple bruises under his yellow skin, he handed the picture back and said, "That one's as good as any, I reckon." In the end, Jesus was whatever you wanted him to be, and it didn't really matter much what he looked like.

"Hold on there a minute," Bill said when Farrell started to walk off. He shut off his truck and took a dry, ragged breath. "Look, Farrell, I know I did you wrong," he said, "and I wish to God I could take it back, but I can't."

Looking toward the store, Farrell could see Hank standing at the front window watching them. It was a sunny day in early November and just then a flock of geese flew over, their dark wings beating against a bright blue sky. As their squawks faded into the distance, Farrell realized that he didn't feel like hating anyone today. "My granddad used to say that everything happens for a reason," he told Bill. "Claimed it was the only thing that kept him from going crazy whenever he thought about all them men he saw killed in the war." He shook his head and shrugged. "But then he went nuts anyway, so I don't know."

"I still wish I hadn't done it," Bill said.

Farrell nodded. "I know you do."

Bill held the picture up. His eyes were foggy from the pain medication. "I don't think I can build this thing by myself," he said. "Shoot, I can't hardly hold a hammer up nowadays."

Farrell went around to the other side of the truck and got in. A bottle of pills lay on the seat along with an envelope on which a list of materials had been scrawled in pencil: plywood, two-by-fours, nails, paint. "I'll help you any way I can," he said.

"I need to get this thing right," Bill said as they started toward town. "I ain't ready to go yet, but the damn doctors have give clear up on me."

The wooden Jesus turned out twelve foot tall, with a brown robe and chalky white face and pink hands turned up like he was asking for a favor or maybe just wondering how in the hell he ever ended up with blond hair and blue eyes. Farrell did most of the work while Bill sat in a chair by a space heater and watched. They did a nice job, but after her husband died, Wilma started fancying it up with Christmas lights and strings of silver garland. As Farrell now pulled away from the stop sign at the end of the holler, he tapped the horn. Wilma turned and waved and Tom threw back his head in a big grin. Cindy stared straight ahead, didn't even let on that she'd even noticed them.

It was nearly dark by the time they reached the cemetery. Farrell grabbed the wreath out of the back of the van, and Cindy followed him in her flimsy shoes across the frozen grass to Charley's spot. Their own monuments were on each side of his, plain, squat stones that already seemed to be sinking a bit into the ground. He laid the wreath on Charley's grave, and Cindy knelt down beside him. As soon as he finished saying a little prayer, she began crying. He patted her on the shoulder and stood up. "Take your time," he said. "I won't be far."

Farrell walked halfway across the cemetery and sat down on a concrete bench just a few yards away from Bill's resting place. The wind picked up a little. As he watched dry brown leaves scuttle between the rows of headstones, he began running the night that Charley died through his head again. Then, inevitably, he thought back to the day he hurt himself jerking on that white-faced cow in Clarence's muddy barn lot. Six months after the accident, he was at the doctor's again, trying to explain a new problem.

"You mean not at all?" the doctor said.

Farrell shook his head. "My wife gets all over me, but it won't do nothing."

"Well, let's take a look."

After a couple minutes of pulling and tugging, the doctor stood up and rubbed his chin, told Farrell that he'd probably damaged some nerves. He handed him a bottle of vitamin pills and a jar of white salve dipped out of a gallon jug. "Rub some of this on your nuts twice a day," the doctor said. "And go buy you some dirty magazines."

"What good is that gonna do?" Farrell asked.

"Take a look at the pictures right before you plan on having any intercourse," the doctor said. "Go over to the newsstand on Main Street and tell the guy working there that I sent you. He's got some stuff under the counter that might do the trick."

Farrell did as instructed, but the problem wouldn't go away. He even went back and bought more magazines, a big box of special stuff from overseas that cost him an entire paycheck. Fortunately, he'd already knocked Cindy up by the time he'd hurt himself. A year or so after Charley was born, she moved into the spare bedroom, claimed it made things easier. Though Farrell had a bad feeling about the arrangement, he didn't argue. It was a relief not having to make excuses every night.

To his surprise, their marriage went pretty smooth right up until Charley entered high school. Then one evening, when Farrell came home from work, Cindy told him she was going out with a couple women she'd met at a Tupperware party over in Bourneville. "Just gonna have a couple drinks, that's all," she said. She was wearing new clothes he'd never seen before. "Be home before midnight," she promised. The next morning he found her sprawled on the couch, her thick black hair stinking of cigarettes, her green eyes bloodshot from screwdrivers. It took her all day to get over the hangover. He thought maybe she'd gotten her fill. But two nights later, she came out of her bedroom wearing another new outfit. His supper was sitting cold on the stove. She was just getting started.

After Charley bought the Mustang, he started staying away at night, too. He was no longer interested in looking at the stars or doing much of anything else with Farrell for that matter. Sitting in the trailer by himself, Farrell sometimes got the old magazines out from the hiding place under his bed. He flipped through the trashy pages hoping for a miracle. But every time he did it, he just ended up picturing Cindy lying beneath some stranger, her legs wrapped around a strong back. One night he took a butcher knife from a drawer in the kitchen and walked out to the garden. He unzipped his pants and laid the cold blade against his skin. He stood there for a long time, his eyes blurry with tears. The next morning he went back over to the garden and pulled the knife out of the apple tree.

One Friday evening, as he listened to Cindy dancing around in her bedroom, putting on her makeup, he decided to follow her. Charley had gone to a basketball game with some of his buddies. She was humming a song when she went out the door. Farrell sat in the kitchen with his keys in his hand until he heard her leave. Driving straight into town, she parked her car on Water Street and hurried into the Hideaway Lounge. An hour later, Farrell saw her walk out of the bar with Bill Watson, his hand on her ass. They got in Bill's old pickup, and he watched them lock lips before they took off. Farrell sat there numb for a few minutes, watching the traffic light at the corner change colors over and over. He'd imagined a hundred different men with his wife over the last couple years, but never his sloppy, whiskey-swilling, red-faced neighbor. On the way back home, he stopped in the middle of Schott's Bridge and puked his supper over the rail into Paint Creek. Charley was sitting on the porch steps huddled in his coat when Farrell pulled in the driveway.

"Out looking for her?" the boy asked. He took a cigarette from his pocket and tapped it against the palm of his hand, then lit it. The smell of beer was on his breath.

Ignoring the question, Farrell glanced up at the cold December sky. "There's Pegasus," he said.

"Fuck Pegasus," Charley said, his voice filling with anger. "I can tell you who the sonofabitch is. I followed them to his house the other night. Some tall, skinny bastard drives a white Oldsmobile."

"I don't need to know," Farrell told his son, trying to keep his voice steady. He should have figured that Bill wasn't the only one.

Charley shook his head, took another drag off the cigarette. "Jesus Christ, old man, don't be such a chickenshit," he said. "Hell, she ain't nothing but a goddamn tramp. Everybody in the county talks about her."

Farrell was standing at the bottom of the steps when he drew back and slapped the boy. Sparks flew in the air and the cigarette landed in a bed of dead flowers. "Don't you ever call your mother anything like that again," he said. "You don't know a damn thing about it." Charley stood up and stepped around his father, headed for his car. Though he took off slow, Farrell heard him punch the accelerator and burn some rubber when he turned onto Black Run. He was still waiting on the boy to come home when the deputy knocked on the door, told him about the wreck.

Getting up from the cold bench, he started back over to Charley's grave. Cindy was still on her knees, smoothing the wreath with her hands. Her teeth were chattering from the cold. "Come on now," Farrell said, helping her up, "we better go before you catch pneumonia." She held onto his arm as they walked back to the van. Once inside, he flipped on the radio, twisted the dial until he found *The Gospel Hour*. When they reached the left turn up into the holler, Farrell looked over and saw all the lights lit up on the wooden Jesus in front of Wilma's house. He pulled off onto the gravel shoulder, shut off the headlights, put the van in park. "What's wrong?" Cindy said.

"Nothing," Farrell said. "I just want to look here a minute." The bulbs wrapped around the Savior were blue and white. An orange electric cord hung out the kitchen window, snaked through the grass over to a plug-in behind the painted sandals. Another song started up on *The Gospel Hour*, something about the glories of Heaven, and how they're all around us right here on Earth if we just open up our hearts to them. Farrell glanced over at his wife. The Jesus lights coming through the windshield softened her face a little, erased some of the trouble from her brow, the gray from her hair. Sometimes he wished that he'd lied to Cindy that morning when she finally came home after being out all night with Bill; maybe told her that Charley had stopped in after the ballgame and fixed himself a sandwich, drank a glass of milk; that he and Farrell had sat in the kitchen and talked and joked around for a while; that when he left, their son had said he was just going for a little ride, promised to be back before midnight. Farrell might have even believed it himself by now.

"We didn't put out nothing for him to eat," Cindy said, when his hand touched hers. A shadow walked past the window in Wilma's kitchen, and a few seconds later all the lights went out on the wooden Jesus. In the darkness, Farrell could see the stars. He looked up to find Pegasus, flying upside down, the way he always does. Then he leaned back in his seat as the song on the radio ended in a long trembling of voices.

Psalm 96

Sing to the Lord a new song—of men and women riding
the last bus home through quarries and yellowing
tobacco fields of Highway 421. Sing the long sigh
and slow grind of axels and tired eyes that watch
through glass the memory of Guthrie and Bluff Hills
and the Greenback Labor Party that never had a chance to
sing of strong arms and backs that broke in heat and boys
and girls who'd grow barefoot through stones and stagnant
water and bellies swole with hunger. Sing malaria, pellagra
and the scars that faded and the scars that didn't. Sing
a new song from the old, the way things work their way
like hookworm up and in through cracks in the skin. Sing
their descendents up from the dust to work in Michigan
auto plants and down to dust again in mines of West Virginia.
Sing cornbread and potatoes. Sing food stamps and long lines
and the water shut-off notice on the door. Sing thirst and stink
and the boys signed up to fight through mustard gas and jungle,
the beaches of Europe and the Philippines, the deserts
of the Middle East. Sing of IEDs and what freedom really means
to empty bellies and an anger at everything. Sing of sand—
how it gets everywhere—hair, the pits of your arms, groin,
grinding away the skin—like hunger gets everywhere. How
sometimes the only thing to put in an empty hand is another
hand. Sing anger and lust and football on cold Friday nights—
the crush of bodies on bodies. Sing full-contact and sex
in muscle cars on back country roads and in the basements
and parking lots. Sing of children and more children. 99 cent
burgers and cold fries and grease that fills them. Sing the grease
that makes the stomach clamp. And single mothers who learned
from their mothers whose men were gone before they were gone,
even when they were there. Sing cosmetology school, beauty

school and the community college down the road. Because
you're 50 years old and still trying, still singing—man gone,
kids trying to be gone and you stealing hours on the nursing home
computer where you work, wiping asses and cleaning bedpans
so you can take a night class on Gender Issues, so you can learn
words like *patriarchy, hegemony, abject, subaltern.* Sing
the privilege you're supposed to have. Sing the spirit. Sing
to the Lord because the Lord is hope that maybe a new song
can rise, green and leafy, from a bitter soil. Sing because it's all
you have—this life bound up in other lives before you
that matter because you say they do, you say you do
because you sing.

FOUR

HOME AND AWAY

To the Young Man Living on the Fourteenth Floor, Missing the Hills of Appalachia

Perhaps you chose this high-rise for the view,
hoping, like back home, to catch sight of a herd
of white-tailed deer slipping through the woods
to drink at the pond, or maybe you wanted to soar
above the landscape like a red-tailed hawk crying
for home, looking for meat to sustain you.

Whatever your plan, you have called to say
they are tearing down the trees, bulldozers razing
the green you love so well, to build a discount store.
And the landlord surprised you by taking out
your door to the balcony, replacing it with solid glass
to cut heating costs midwinter.

You still have a window, I remind you, and a lake
not far away. Trees, though scattered
through suburban yards, hold birds and squirrels,
change colors just the same. And the next time
you move because the walls keep getting closer,
look for a place facing south; I'll be there, waving.

The Stars in Shawnee

Only early June, but the heat feels like August. Eleanor and Shelby sit on the front steps of the old Victorian-style house in downtown Los Angeles, drinking homemade margaritas and watching the daylight drain away to dusk. Shelby slaps a mosquito away from her sweat-sticky thigh. She has long thin arms and skinny ankles and wire-straight hair that sometimes looks brown and sometimes looks auburn, depending on the light.

"Damn it," she says.

"What?" Eleanor has full eyebrows and a tiny diamond stud in her left nostril. She favors sundresses and wears her hair pinned up with silver barrettes. In high school a boy told her that she had "perfect breasts" because they fit perfectly in his hands like two firm oranges. Now she thinks of him every time she eats an orange.

"I meant to stop at the 7-Eleven," Shelby says. "I wanted to buy a lotto ticket."

Eleanor checks her watch. "You'd better hurry, if you want to get it before the drawing. It's almost six now."

Shelby swats at the air. "Naw, it's okay. I don't feel like walking."

"I can drive you," Eleanor says.

"You can't drive."

"I can drive." She holds up her margarita cup. "This is only my second."

"It's fine. There's always next week," Shelby says, working her fingers through her hair to massage her scalp, searching for lumps. She is terrified of dying. So terrified that she sometimes thinks she might as well kill herself and get it over with.

Eleanor gazes out at the pink smear of sunset caught between buildings. "There aren't really sunsets in L.A.," she says. "Daylight just . . . slips away." She is thinking of Shawnee. As a child she would sometimes grow anxious, gazing up at the full expanse of sky, trying to grasp where it ended. Ohio sky isn't like L.A. sky. Ohio sky doesn't end. It stretches at the horizons to a blurred uncertain line. So much sky. Two years ago, when she first moved to L.A., Eleanor would sometimes spend hours online, clicking through photographs of cornfields and rivers. But you can't capture the sky in a photograph, not truly. The sky is what she misses most.

"If I won the lottery," Shelby says, "I would buy this house so we didn't have to pay rent all the time. Paying rent sucks."

"You'd buy this house?" Eleanor asks. "This house of all houses?"

Shelby half-turns to gaze at the eaves, paint peeling like a bad sunburn. "I've grown fond of it, I guess," she says. "I like this porch. And the music-note wallpaper in the hallway. And I like how the honeysuckle grows up under my window."

"My window doesn't get honeysuckle," Eleanor says.

"Plus, if I bought it, it would be mine. That would be enough to make me love it."

"Then you could live anywhere, is what you're saying. As long as you own the house you live in. You can love anywhere."

"I guess so," Shelby says. She takes a pondering sip of margarita. Inside her room, on her bedside table, rests a bottle of pills and a glass of water. "But I do really like this house."

Eleanor stretches her legs out in front of her. She hasn't shaved in a couple days and dark nubby hairs are visible on her knees and shins. The heat makes her legs itch. "If I won the lottery, I wouldn't live in L.A.," she says. "I'd buy a house somewhere far away."

"Where?"

"I don't know. A small town somewhere."

"Let me guess: Shawnee?"

"I'm just saying, Shel. Someplace people actually know your name. Around here, you say hi and people look at you like you're crazy."

"But is it really like that in Shawnee?" Shelby asks. "Everyone's friendly? Everyone bakes casseroles and apple pies?"

"My mom makes green bean casserole."

"No pie?"

"Well, sometimes, on holidays." Eleanor leans back on her elbows. She knows Shelby is making fun of her, but she takes the bait anyway. "Pecan pie. My Aunt Susan makes the best pecan pie. She won a ribbon at the county fair."

"The county fair!"

"What's wrong with the county fair?"

"Nothing's wrong," Shelby says. "It just sounds . . . quaint."

"L.A. has a fair, doesn't it?"

"Not a quaint little county fair, that's for sure."

Eleanor wrenches a pack of Malboros from her jeans pocket. Shelby watches Eleanor search her other pockets for her lighter. There are so many ways to die. Lung cancer. Skin cancer. Fire. Car crash. So many uncontrollable ways. Shelby exhales a drawn-out sigh that turns into a yawn. "God," she says. "I hate paying rent. I feel like all my money goes towards rent. I mean, all my money."

"That's for sure." Eleanor, lighter found, tips her pack and daintily pulls out a cigarette with the tips of two fingers. "Do you mind?" she asks Shelby.

"Of course not," Shelby says. "You don't have to ask."

Eleanor smokes when she's stressed and when she drinks. Tonight, she is both stressed and drinking. This afternoon brought yet another no-call-back in a long string of call-backs she hasn't gotten. She didn't expect it to be this hard. Everyone said it would take time, and yes, she expected it to take some time—but *two years*? Two years and nothing more than a handful of student films and background bit parts and one shitty half-line ("Mmm, cinnamon") in a gum commercial? Sometimes the embarrassment felt so big it eclipsed everything else. Her identity nothing more than a tired cliché: the small-town Midwest girl who moves to L.A. to become an actress, squeezing in auditions between her double-shifts as a waitress. Everyone was tired of that story. Especially Eleanor. *If I don't land something in the next three months*, she thinks now, *I'm moving back home and getting a real job*. She turns her face to blow the smoke away from Shelby. She knows cigarette smoke gives Shelby a headache, even though Shelby, a jubilant martyr, makes a point not to complain.

Shelby gulps her margarita. She shifts her body slightly away from Eleanor's but doesn't say anything, trying not to think about the second-hand smoke wafting into her lungs. She believes friends make sacrifices for each other. She believes sacrifices are what make friendships stronger. Like a bird culling thread and twigs to build a nest, but in reverse. Casting away in order to build.

Eleanor takes a drag of her cigarette, thinking of her high school friend Bella, who taught her to smoke. They haven't talked in six years. Eleanor believes friendships are a matter of convenience and circumstance. Eventually, she or Shelby will move away. Drift apart. Get sick of each other. And then this, all of this—the margaritas, the lotto tickets, the lazy spirals of conversation—will end. It is inevitable. None of Eleanor's friendships have lasted as long as she had wanted them to. Eleanor is careful to turn her face away from Shelby when she exhales, so as not to speed up the decline.

"Hey Eleanor?" Shelby says suddenly. "If I buy a lotto ticket and it's a winner, I want to split some of the money with you."

"Thanks, Shel. That's sweet."

"No, seriously. Listen. If I die or something, like before I get the winnings, make sure you get some, okay? Don't let my parents take all the money."

Eleanor leans back on her elbows. The clouds, limned with purple, look bruised. All the ice in her margarita has melted. "Okay, Shel," she says. "What's wrong?"

"Nothing." Last week, Shelby took the bottle of painkillers from her medicine cabinet and placed them on her bedside table. Every morning when she wakes up, the pills are the first thing she sees. When she drives home from work in the evening, she considers how easy it would be to turn the wheel ever so slightly, to lean into oncoming traffic like lovers lean towards each other at a cocktail party.

"Come on," Eleanor says.

Shelby sighs. Her fingers thread through her hair and massage her scalp. "I think," she says, "that I'm gonna die soon."

If Eleanor were not Eleanor but someone else, she might laugh uncomfortably and change the subject. Or she might think Shelby is being purposefully melodramatic and try to brush it away with facts: she is only twenty-two, she eats healthy greens, she wears her seatbelt. If Eleanor were Shelby's mother, she would jump straight to alarm and ask what's wrong, is she depressed, is she eating enough?

But Eleanor is Eleanor. She tips ash from her cigarette into the rosebushes and asks, "Why?"

Shelby stretches out her legs, almost knocking over her empty plastic cup. "I've just been thinking about it a lot lately. Death. It's always . . . there. At the back of my mind. It didn't used to be there. I mean, it was there sometimes, I guess, but not that often. Not always like it is now."

"What's changed?"

"I don't know," Shelby says. She didn't expect it to be like this. Everyone said she would be a good teacher. She thought she could actually make a difference, even a small difference, even to just one kid. But she is a failure. Her students all hate her. When she turns to write on the whiteboard they whisper and titter to each other, and when she poses questions for discussion they stare at her blankly. No one raises a hand. Middle school kids are supposed to like their teachers. English is supposed to be a subject the kids look forward to. There are no wrong answers in English class. If you don't have something to say you can make something up. It's not like she has been assigning much homework, either—just the typical vocabulary exercises and a book report every other month.

"Did I ever tell you about my Death Dream?" Eleanor asks.

"No," Shelby says.

"When I was in seventh grade, I had a recurring dream that I drowned. There was this pond by my house that I used to swim in a lot. I loved it there. But in my dream, this whirlpool started in the center of the pond, and no matter how hard I swam for the shore, I felt myself being pulled under the water." Eleanor remembers the fear that gripped her chest and limbs as her dream-lungs filled with water. She hadn't felt calm like everyone says you feel right before you die. She felt panicked and scared.

"I was terrified to go to sleep because I died every night in my dream," Eleanor continues. "Finally my parents took me to a shrink."

Shelby frowns. "I thought you couldn't die in a dream. I read somewhere that if you die in your dream, then you actually die for real in your sleep."

"There's no way they could know that," Eleanor says. "You can't know what someone was dreaming when they died."

"I'm just saying, I read it somewhere. In a magazine."

"Well, I died in my dream."

"So what happened?" Shelby asks. "Did you go to Heaven?"

"No, it was just dark. Dark and quiet. And then I'd wake up." Eleanor stubs out her cigarette. She drops the butt into her empty plastic cup. "Anyway, it stopped after a couple months. The shrink said it was tied to my parents' divorce."

A fly hovers around their sticky cups. Shelby swats it away. "See, that makes sense," she says. "Part of what scares me is I can't think of a trigger. There's no reason I should be obsessing about death."

Eleanor sits quietly. She is the type of person who can keep eye contact for a long time. Shelby is the type of person who gets uncomfortable and looks away.

Shelby looks away. "I figure it means I'm gonna die soon," she says. "It's a premonition."

"Maybe it's the opposite," Eleanor says. "Like how a watched pot never boils."

"Huh." With her index finger, Shelby lightly traces around the small scar on her thigh she got from climbing a chain-link fence in grade school. There were no trees, so Shelby climbed fences. "You mean, I won't die if I'm too busy thinking about dying."

"Yeah, I guess." Eleanor smiles like a lady in an old painting. Her lips aren't really smiling, but her eyes are.

"What?" Shelby says. "What are you thinking about?"

"Nothing."

"Are you laughing at me? You're laughing at me."

"No, Shel," Eleanor says. "I was just thinking of my shrink."

"Your shrink?"

"Of what my shrink would say."

"What shrink?" Shelby leans forward, elbows on knees. "You don't go to a shrink."

"My old shrink, the one my parents sent me to. Because of my Death Dream."

"Oh," Shelby says. "What would he say?" The sky is steadily losing color. Above them, the moon is an orange.

Eleanor lights another cigarette. The moon is a perfect breast. "She would say, the question becomes: if you're constantly worried about death, are you really living?"

"No." Shelby rubs her eyes. "That's the answer, right? 'No, so I should stop worrying and start living!' Right?"

"There's no answer. It's just what my shrink would say."

"Do you think she's right?" Shelby asks. "Is that the answer?"

Eleanor exhales, a perfect trail of gray smoke. She doesn't say anything.

Her recurring dream wasn't really because of her parents' divorce. Her parents had been fighting bitterly for months. The divorce wasn't much of a surprise.

Eleanor first dreamt of drowning on a Wednesday in late November. That day, her best friend Mariah Quinn inexplicably untangled herself from Eleanor and retangled herself with Veronica Cross. "Sorry, Eleanor," she said. "Bus seats only hold two." Seventh-grade Eleanor walked numbly to the back of the bus and slumped down in her seat, hiding behind her backpack, crying tears into her lunchbag. She and Mariah had been best friends since kindergarten, when they both caught the chickenpox at the same time. They sat next to each other on the bus, ate lunch together, had slumber parties on the weekends. How quickly everything could be swept away.

Eleanor leans sideways against the porch railing. Between the clamor of buildings, a few stars press through the smoggy night sky. Suddenly, she points. "Hey, Shel. Make a wish."

"I thought you only wish on shooting stars," Shelby says, thinking of Bobby Meyers, the lanky blonde boy her teenage self wished for and wished for.

"In L.A., you should wish on any star you can find," Eleanor says.

Shelby tilts her face up to the sky. In ninth grade, she wore the same blue polka-dotted headband for two months because she was wearing it when Bobby Meyers asked for her phone number, and some part of her thought he would only call if she kept wearing it. The white polka-dots gradually turned gray, and then the cloth at the ends of headband began to fray and unravel from the plastic. Shelby stopped wearing it. Bobby Meyers never called. Still, Shelby knows she will keep the bottle of pills and the glass of water on her bedside table, a comfort, a superstition, like the dreamcatcher hanging above Eleanor's bed across the hall.

"We do too have stars in L.A.," Shelby says, pointing. "Look! Right there."

"Those aren't real stars," Eleanor says. "Not like Shawnee. You should see the stars in Shawnee."

The night before she left for L.A. to become a famous actress, Eleanor slept outside in the bed of her dad's pickup truck. She found the Big Dipper and Orion's Belt and searched the sky for shooting stars. None came. Or perhaps the sky was too big, and she missed them.

Reading James Wright during a Louisiana Afternoon Thunderstorm I Realize There Are Worse Places to Live Than Zanesville, Ohio

On the Gulf, thunderstorms rumble. I sit by the porch window, watch water race off a gutterless roof. A small pond will pool below between cypress tree roots, well up over sidewalks. This is nothing like the Ohio River's clay waters that carry coal barges between tree branches. It's rainwater drainage and a place for bridges to cross. I'm wrong to stay here among suspicious Cajuns who wonder how I ended up here, something I wonder too.

Citywide concrete canals flush runoff into the Vermillion, but in Zanesville, a Y-bridge crosses the Muskingum and the Licking, lets motorists decide which part of Zanesville to avoid—closed auto parts factories or creeks scattered with broken tile.

Down here, rusty bridge truss after bridge truss rises up to sea level for shrimpers, back down for flatbed trucks full of oil drilling pipes, oil rig platform parts, and sugarcane stalks. The one semester I taught at a Catholic high school, a sign on LA 193 near Abbeville read *Teens say no to sex and yes to a future.*

As a teenager, I drove past sagging barns and plowed cornfields, even further out of town than my parents' subdivision house, went off blazed trails at Black Hand Gorge, past overgrown canal locks, towards a tunnel that traveled through a hill by long-gone track. When could I ever take a train to Columbus?

Before internal combustion and interstates, water was the swiftest way out. It was easy to ride it down to New Orleans on the Mississippi. Even Lincoln tried it. Now, rivers seem like just something else to notice through dusty car windows.

A Ride

Sweet corn just papyrus shocks now along the roadside,
knotted clumps of tomato vines,
the river a rippled brown margin glinting back
low angles of sun that make everything look clear.
Summer was too long. We live too far south.
But winding over the small hills on the Kentucky side of the water
I can take in this late October ease like breaths of ripe air
tinged with the dust smell of leaf piles and apples stacked at the fruit stand.

Tell me, Nostalgia, how many memories are we making today
as Anna and Teddy scramble down the pumpkin hill again,
each orange globe a shout against the fading grass?
A wasp plunders a bruised winesap by the turban squash.
Videotape hums in the camcorders as minivans load and depart,
full of gourds and domesticity, for the blond suburbs.
Lugging our sacks, I am fatherly, autumnal.

I remember the soft pleasure in these cycles that never seem to change,
how it rests on the kids playing Twenty Questions in the backseat,
in the light catching a swirl of my wife's hair above her cheekbone.
Through the windshield the peeling township post office and the shacks
staggering toward the river
are a genre painting. On the far hills fat sheaves of burley
cure in the black half-open tobacco barns.

When we reach the ferry, the river's yellowed with the sunset.
The auburn shag and watery eyes of the ferryman
gleam like the final product of a dozen generations.
Sixteen, happy to be employed, he spins the big iron wheel,
leaps like a dancer from the tug to the barge and back.

The Friday Night Dance

Like some boys, I could not fast dance. It wasn't that I didn't have rhythm or coordination. Instead, I was restricted by not wanting to make a fool out of myself—a guiding principle that I thought would carry me throughout my life.

I admired those who could fast dance—Dick, Butch, Gary, Tom, Mick, and Rodney. What these guys could do was recognized by all of the girls and they wanted to be slung around by them—you could see it in the girls' faces, even at a distance. There was no way that such interest by girls was going to happen for me. I just couldn't break out of my shell. I was forever standing around the outside of the inbounds line of the high school gym—watching.

It was true that for the last two years there had been sporadic parties at someone's house—a birthday or just a hangout. Most of these events were closely supervised by parents and as such were innocent. When I was eleven, some of the get-togethers featured spin the bottle, where the object was to break the ice and get kids to dance together using a spinning bottle to select the couples. Once, I was lucky enough to be matched with a girl named Sharon.

I had never held a girl the way you do when you slow dance together, but Sharon was experienced and very patient with my awkwardness and my stiff, mechanical movement. We danced to Rosemary Clooney, Patti Page, and Doris Day.

Gradually, my embarrassment and discomfort grew to a pleasant acceptance and my rigor mortis became a little more dance-like. Sharon nurtured me through all of my agitation about dancing and holding a girl, albeit at arm's length. When the fast music came on, though, I sat down and watched.

You want me to cast a fly rod with twenty yards of line out behind me—OK; you want me to catch a fly ball behind my back, then I'm your guy. But if you want me to flap my arms and kick my feet and be responsible for throwing a girl around on the dance floor . . . well, I'll be over here in the corner with my fly rod and my Rawlings glove. Sharon could not help me through this one.

By the time I was thirteen, I still had the same attitude about fast dancing, although slow dancing was now not only acceptable, but also part of my talents. The parties, however, became less about breaking the ice and dancing and more about other acquired skills. A new twist was added to spin the bottle: Kissing.

A kiss up to this point was a cute sign of affection—something pecked on the cheek of your mother or aunts. I had seen my mother and dad kiss on the lips, but that was reserved for grown-ups. It was their way of expressing love for one another—after all, they were married.

But kids were kids. While you might be tight with your buddies, there were no girls that you were tight with—certainly none that you would kiss. Heck, I was blood relations with my girl cousins, and I certainly wouldn't kiss them! So, this new version of spin the bottle raised my anxiety level.

One night, while at Melinda's house, a girl named Freda stood in the center of a rough circle of my schoolmates who were sitting in chairs and stools or lounging on the floor. Freda was going to be in the seventh grade, but she was dressed older with a gray circle skirt, a white blouse, and a pink scarf tied around her neck. She reached down and spun the bottle.

While I had hoped that the barrel of that glass gun would miss me, I was the first one it aimed at. The crowd went "OOOh," and everyone demanded that I kiss Freda on the lips. I didn't know her. I had no affection for her. It made me nervous to pucker up and press her lips with mine with everyone watching. But I had to.

So I got up and approached her. We both leaned over at the waist with our hands to our side. Our eyes met and then I saw hers close. She smelled of Wrigley's Juicy Fruit gum. Our noses hit. Our heads retreated slightly and her eyes opened. We both immediately recognized the problem but chose the same direction to angle our heads (this was really awkward). The room remained dead quiet while Freda and I worked out the head rotation without saying a word.

Her eyes closed. Juicy Fruit . . . kiss . . . soft . . . press . . . breathe . . . soft . . . pull back. Her eyes slowly opened and she smiled. She smiled! I must have done OK. Weelllll. Not so bad after all. I'd do that again!

The steel mill was the major industry in the area. Over 4,000 people worked there, most of them members of the United Steelworkers of America. The relationship of the union to management was a tricky one, one that seemed ready to break at any time.

One day at Shorty's Barbershop while I was waiting for a haircut, the men were talking about the union history of the mill. How in 1912, there was a pitched battle between company men and union men with both sides having guns. There was even a machine gun up on the hill across from the Blast Furnace. In the 1930s, the competing unions and the management were all battling with each other using baseball bats and rocks and set fires.

Of course, in 1952 there was the National Steel Strike, which was very bad for everyone. Even my dad, who was a meat cutter and wasn't a member of the union, complained because it slowed down the meat business at Schaeffer's Grocery Store where he worked, as people bought cheaper canned goods rather than fresh-cut beef or chicken.

When times were good, though, both the union and management would do a lot for the town. Among the things that the union did was to sponsor dances for teenagers at the Union Hall. Sometimes, the dances were on Saturday afternoons and, sometimes, they were scheduled for Friday evenings. The Friday Night Dance started at six o'clock and would end at nine o'clock. Because I was finished with my paper route around five-thirty, and because the Union Hall was on my paper route, it was easy for me to make the dance.

I had cleared it with Mother and Dad and told them that I was going to go and would be home by ten o'clock. (While they preferred nine o'clock, they allowed ten o'clock to see how dependable I was. I was determined to be home early to show them that they could trust me.) It was going to be an eventful night.

After passing out papers, I stopped at Blackburn's Market for a baloney sandwich, a Royal Crown Cola, and a bag of Tip Top Potato Chips. Then I went on to the Steelworkers Hall.

Teenagers were showing up from all over—from East High School, West High School, Portsmouth High School, Minford, Clay, Valley, Wheelersburg, Notre Dame, and Glenwood High School, where I would be in the eighth grade when school started.

By six o'clock, the parking lot was full of waxed and polished cars— Studebakers, Chevrolets, Pontiacs, Oldsmobiles, Fords, Mercurys, Plymouths,

Desotos, Dodges, even a Kaiser. They were all American-made cars—no one would have parked a foreign car in the Steelworkers Hall lot.

The hall itself was on the street level, as were the offices for the union leadership. In the basement was a kitchen, a bar, vending machines, a recreation room, restrooms, lockers, and more offices.

For the dance, there were five union members who served as chaperones. The union had hired a local disc jockey to spin records, four police officers to look mean and keep order, and a kitchen staff of three people who cooked hamburgers, hot dogs, and French fries. They also had an ice cream freezer full of Drumsticks, Fudgsicles, and ice cream cups. All these things were offered at half of what you would pay at a restaurant.

I went in and headed downstairs to leave my paper route things—carrier bag, wire cutter, paper punch, collection ring. They were stowed in a locker with no lock, which was OK because no one ever took other people's belongings, fearful that the union would stop having dances if there were trouble. For the same reason, there were no fights in the hall. Fights seemed to start in the parking lot where some guy would wait for another kid and then they would take it to the alley behind the hall.

I had purposefully thought about what I would wear—which was unusual for me. I wanted to look good, so I wore my new khakis, a blue button-down shirt, and saddle oxfords that were black-and-white. A few combs of the hair and then up the stairs to who knew what.

The hall was big and wide and open with a high ceiling—it was a place that could hold perhaps a thousand people seated on folding chairs. There was a stage at one end where the disc jockey played his 45-rpm records. Nearby, a stern-looking police officer stood glaring at the crowd. The floor was wooden, like a basketball court.

Some kids were standing and others sitting around the walls right and left. Dancing was in the middle. Talking generally happened at the back of the hall where you entered because there was less noise back there.

Everybody was well dressed, not like Sunday church clothes, but like me. The girls had dresses that were pleated or round with lots of slips or petticoats or whatever they were called underneath. Most of the guys were dressed in khakis or dark slacks, although there were a few that looked like "hoods"—white T-shirts, Levi's with pegged cuffs, studded black belts with big buckles, and black motorcycle boots with taps that clicked when they walked. They all had wet-looking, slick-backed hair. Even the shorter guys in that crowd looked tough and acted tougher; I decided to avoid them.

Big cabinet speakers were on the stage with the disc jockey and the policeman. They projected the music to the crowd of dancers. Of the two hundred kids that were there, at least half of them were dancing. If girls wanted to dance but didn't have a boy to dance with, they would dance with each other. When a song was over, everybody clapped.

My friend John, a really good baseball player, came over and stood next to me; we watched. Even if you weren't dancing—like us—watching the dancers made you smile. It made me envious, too, but I knew that I couldn't do it.

The disc jockey seemed to have a routine of three fast songs to one slow song:

Bill Haley & His Comets	"Rock around the Clock"
Little Richard	"Tutti Frutti"
Chuck Berry	"Maybelline"
The Platters	"Only You"
Ray Charles	"I've Got a Woman"
The Crew-Cuts	"Ko Ko Mo"
Fats Domino	"Ain't That a Shame"

I decided that I was not going to let the night go by without dancing. I was looking for Sharon, since she was pretty and could tolerate my woodenness, but she wasn't there. I spotted Freda. I had never danced with Freda, but we had "kissed," so she was at least familiar with me.

The Penguins began singing "Earth Angel" at 45 revolutions per minute. "O, O, O . . . *wah-wah-wah*, O, O, O . . ."

"Hi, Freda. Remember me—Ron? I was wondering if you would like to dance?"

For a moment, it looked like she was considering her options.

"*Oooo*," the Penguins crooned.

"Yes, I would like that," she answered unenthusiastically, probably because no other suitor appeared. But nevertheless, I had opened my mouth and she said "yes," so I wanted to make it worth her while by paying attention to her.

We assumed the position with a nice comfortable space between us. She smelled of Juicy Fruit chewing gum and a perfume like my mother's—Emeraude?

The Penguins were seriously sentimental.

"So, Freda, are you ready for school to start?" I asked, while shuffling, 1-2-3-pause, 1-2-3-pause, just as Sharon had taught me.

"Weeelll," she said, "this was the first year that I bought all my school clothes. My mom and I used to argue about it all the time and she would dress me like she wanted to see me, but that was not how I wanted to dress, so . . ."

The Penguins "ooohed."

I shuffled, 1-2-3-pause, listening to Freda.

" . . . so, Mother just threw up her hands finally and said that she would give me the money to shop for myself . . ."

The Penguins had more questions.

I didn't.

"So, we caught the bus downtown. Now, when my mother goes downtown to shop she insists on wearing a hat and gloves. Why? I have no idea. I tried to . . ." Freda continued.

The Penguins were musically earnest.

"So we shopped at Martings, Bragdons, Kobackers, and then J.C. Penney's with Mom in her hat and gloves. I couldn't believe how many . . ." (1-2-3-pause, 1-2-3-pause, 1-2-3-pause).

The Penguins had visions.

"So, I got seven different outfits and my mom had to admit that they looked really good on me, but then there was the matter of shoes, so . . ."

The Penguins confessed.

"So, the shoes were all too expensive at Atlas and it was getting late, but Mom wanted to get this wrapped up, and even though I would never shop there for my clothes, we went to Kresge's Five and Dime where they have the shoes . . ."

The Penguins concluded.

"Thank you, Ron. I had a really good time." Freda concluded.

"Me too," I concluded.

As she went back to her girlfriends, I watched her walk away and thought that she must have gone to Etiquette Class, where they made girls walk with books on their heads and are taught to say "thank you" after a dance. Maybe I should have thanked her. I enjoyed dancing even though she talked so much. Maybe she was so talkative because she was nervous—or maybe she just had a lot to say.

I went back to stand beside John. "How was it?" he asked.

"It was all right," I replied, smiling.

We stood there and watched as dancers went through the Cha-Cha-Cha, the Stroll and the Bunny Hop. I kind of wanted to go slow dance again, but I didn't want to risk asking Freda because it might look like what it wasn't. There was always the chance that she would turn me down, too.

Unexpectedly, the disc jockey announced that the next slow dance would be a "ladies' choice." Apprehension flooded over me. I mean, if a girl asked me to dance and I really didn't want to dance with her, what should I do? Or if two girls approached me, what do I say? I never took Etiquette Class; I didn't know what to do—so I was going to be put into an awkward situation—which I did not like.

Quickly, I stuck a piece of Dentyne chewing gum in my mouth, which Mother had dug out of the bottom of her purse for me. It tasted like face powder at first, but then the spicy flavor came through.

"All right, Ladies," the disc jockey intoned, "I'm going to spin 'Only You' by the Platters next. Now's the time. Make your play for this S-L-O-O-W-W dance 'cause . . . it's Ladies' Choice. Go find your guy!"

There was noise and giddy laughter and feet shuffling on the wooden floor as the girls fanned out to ask a boy to dance. Tension was in the air. Out of a crisscrossing crowd of people going here and there, a pretty girl with nicely tanned skin and dark brown eyes walked straight to me and said, "Will you dance with me?"

John gave me an elbow in the ribs just as I was saying, "Y-EH-ss." I couldn't believe someone that pretty was asking me to dance. She took my hand and led me to the floor.

The Platters began. So did we.

I was holding her to dance the way that I knew and she just glided around as if she were on roller skates. She was looking at me, in my eyes, the whole time. I was almost hypnotized. She never said a word. Neither did I—not that I could. This was something.

The Platters openly confided their feelings.

On the second verse, we were in the same position with the same amount of space between us. But then she eliminated the space! Moving closer, she touched the front of my body with hers, softly.

She had a perfume on that was not my mother's perfume. It was heady and piercing. When we moved, our feet were between each other's. We hadn't said a word. Our hands were sweaty.

1–2-3-pause, 1–2-3-pause.

1–2-3-pause, 1–2-3-pause.

Sometime during the third verse, her head came to rest on my shoulder. Her freshly washed hair smelled like Prell shampoo. We fit together like two pieces of a puzzle. I didn't know her name.

" . . . *yoooooooooooooooooooou,*" *the Platters finished.*

I didn't want them to stop.

There was applause as everyone appreciated the change of pace. She and I backed away from each other, but held each other's eyes. I was shuffling through the deck of cards in my mind, looking for some help as to what I should do next. There was no help. Words were not forming on my lips because there were too many in my mind.

The disc jockey broke the mood. "All right, you cool cats. Here's Bill Haley & His Comets with 'See You Later Alligator.'" The music started as we were still looking at each other. Some instinct caused me to take her hand and lead her to the back of the hall where it was quieter, although still difficult to talk.

"My name's Ron," I managed to say.

She replied in a low, alto voice, "My name's Whila."

"What?" I didn't think I'd heard her correctly. "I thought you said 'Whila.'"

She cupped her hand and leaned towards my ear and said, "W-EYE-la."

"Well . . . uh . . . all right . . . uh," I stuttered. Thankfully, she laughed; so did I.

"I have to be home by eight o'clock," Whila said. "Do you want to walk me home?"

While I thought that the guy was always supposed to make the decisions and determine the direction of events, Whila was in charge here, and although I was a little off balance, things were working out better than I could have planned.

"Sure. That would be great," I said as confidently as possible. "Where do you live?" I asked.

"We just moved into a house on Rhodes Avenue." That wasn't too far away, so off we went. I moved to her side nearest traffic to protect Whila from dirt and mud and splashing water—none of which were there this night—but it's what Mother said I should do when walking with a girl. I did have *some* manners.

I was convinced that the best way to pass time with Whila and show interest in her was to ask her about herself. "Are you from Scioto County?" I offered, thinking that she was from the West Side, maybe.

"My mom and I came here from Columbus. Mom has some relatives here and they thought this would be a better place for us to live than the big city," she said.

"Really? Why's that?"

"Well, my mom and dad got a divorce eighteen months ago and my dad didn't take it well. Mom got the house and custody of me. He is supposed to pay alimony and support, but he doesn't always.

"Soon after the divorce, he would come around and bother her and stuff—call her at two o'clock in the morning, send her nasty things in the mail, just park outside our house, watching. He would show up at my school offering to take me home in his car. The police told him that he wasn't supposed to do that.

"Mom had a job at a bank in Columbus as a teller, and my dad would show up there and make a scene. Mom thought that she could find a job in other places and decided to move. She applied at three banks here and one offered her a job, so here we are. We moved in two days ago and she starts work on Monday."

I began to realize that many average people have interesting stories to tell. "How old are you?" I asked.

"Yeah, I knew this would come up. It's kind of embarrassing—I'm 14, but I'll be 15 next month. I should be in the ninth grade, but I failed the eighth grade in Columbus because of all the stuff with my dad and mom. I'm not dumb; I just missed too many days and couldn't catch up, so here I am, an eighth grader again."

"Well then, we'll be in the same class. That will be nice," keeping a positive tone to the conversation. My Grandmother Borders always said that "the glass is half full, not half empty," and that I should think about everything that way, even when bad things happen. She'll be fifteen when I'm thirteen. OK with me.

"I hope you don't mind me asking," I said, "but I've never heard the name 'Whila' before. Where did that come from?"

"A lot of people never heard that name before and always ask me to repeat it a second time. When I was a kid, I hated it and wanted to be 'Katie' or 'Mary,' or some normal name, but as I get older, I'm beginning to like it more and more, and besides, there's too many Marys. Anyway, my mom grew up in Detroit and her best friend was a girl named Whila. Mom loved her friend so much that she named me after her. I guess Mom's friend is a famous church organist or something. What do people call you?" Whila asked.

"Well, my family calls me 'Ronnie' or 'Ronnie Dean,' but I think that that makes me sound like a three-year-old, so I'm trying to get everybody to call me 'Ron' because that sounds older, I mean my voice changed two years ago."

Whila picked up on the voice. "My voice has gotten hoarse since we moved here last weekend. I don't know what it is. I don't have allergies."

"Could be the mill. You'll get used to it." I advised.

"Here we are. This is our house," she said. "Do you want to come in? . . . Oh, wait, I had better ask my mom." Whila disappeared inside while I stood on the sidewalk.

Her house was brick and appeared to be one room wide with a deep porch, big enough for an aqua-and-ivory glider to sit under the picture window and next to the front door.

"Come on in," said Whila excitedly.

This day was getting very complicated, but I was going to stand up straight as if I knew what I was doing. We went all the way back into the kitchen.

"Ron, this is my mom. Mom, this is Ron."

She was kind of what I thought bank tellers should look like—in the face. What was different was the way she was dressed. She had Levi's on. I really had not seen many women in pants. Her blue jeans were apparently too long because the cuffs were rolled up several times to about where her calf started and she had white canvas tennis shoes on with what looked like a man's white T-shirt tucked into her pants with an orange fabric belt around her thin waist, yet she looked neat and orderly.

"Nice to meet you, Ron. Thanks for walking Whila home. You'll have to forgive the way I look; I've been scrubbing the inside of cabinets. Listen, I'm sure you've worked up an appetite dancing, so why don't you go have a seat in the living room and I'll whip something up for you. Oh, call me Rita."

"Thank you . . . Rita." I looked at Whila for guidance. She motioned me back to the front room where the black-and-white RCA TV was. There was a couch against the long wall and an armchair at an angle that had the best view of the television. So I sat in the armchair for the best angle. Whila, still standing, had something of a disappointed look on her face as she sat down on the couch—alone. I was so inexperienced at this!

"Oh," she said, "I forgot to turn the TV on." And with that, she got up and suggested, "Why don't you sit on the couch—there's no glare on the TV there."

Whila was very clever, I thought. She didn't make me feel like the dope I was and instead found a way to make everything all right. So I moved to the couch and sat next to the arm.

She stayed at the TV while it warmed up—the NBC network came on showing *Truth or Consequences* with Jack Bailey. It was a funny, slapstick kind of program that appealed to people like me who thought a water balloon breaking over someone's head was funny. Whila thought so, too; I could feel her laugh as we sat shoulder to shoulder on the couch together.

Soon, Whila's mom called us into the kitchen. "Nothing fancy, but I hope you like it." Baked split hot dogs filled with Velveeta cheese and wrapped in bacon. Holy cow! It couldn't get much better. We sat down with a bowl of Tom's Potato Chips, four hot dogs, bread, mustard, ketchup and cold seven-ounce bottles of Coke.

"This looks great. Thank you, Rita, so much," I offered. Rita sat at the kitchen table with us. One side of the table was flat against the wall so it was perfect for three people. She had a cup of coffee.

"What do you like to do, Ron?" asked Rita.

"Well, I like to fly-fish, play baseball, and sing. I'd like to learn how to play chess. My paper route kind of eats into my free time, but I have good customers and I am able to have a little money," I said, proud of my life to this point.

"That's very nice, Ron. So, you sing? What do you sing?" Rita continued the questions, keeping me from my hot dog, but I didn't mind.

"I don't sing rock and roll. I like ballads, instead," I said, starting to bring the hot dog to my mouth, but then stopped. I thought that this was going to end up with me singing, so I didn't want to clog up my throat. I was right.

"Can you sing us something?" Rita asked (or challenged, I couldn't tell which).

"Mom!" Whila tried to save me.

"Sure," I said. Now there were a lot of things that I wouldn't do on the spot for fear that I would look bad. But the things I was good at I was happy to show off, because I was a showoff. Quickly, I decided to sing Doris Day's hit "Secret Love."

I cleared my throat. I sang the first stanza slowly and intimately. It was good and I knew it, and I felt sure they would be impressed. I held the last note for a long time, adding vibrato at the end, increasing the impression that I knew what I was doing.

" . . . *freeeeeeeeeeeeeeee.*" I finished.

They both went "Ooooh" and applauded. Now, I felt in charge. It was good.

"Well, Ron, you're welcome back anytime. Take your time and finish up here. I'm going out back to pull some weeds while there is still a little light." Whila was smiling at me, as her mom went out the back door.

"I guess we have a lot to learn about each other," she said, as I was finally getting to enjoy my hot dog. Boy, was it ever good! I didn't want to be a pig, so I only had one.

"Do you want to go out on the porch and sit on the glider?" Whila asked.

I had learned by this point that I shouldn't pass up invitations like that from her. We took our Cokes with us. She stopped in the bathroom and I went on.

The glider apparently came with the house and needed to be oiled because it squeaked badly at each glide, so we tried to be still. There was no place to sit our Cokes, so we finished them and sat the empties on the flat banister railing in front of us. Traffic passed by on Rhodes Avenue. Across the street was the final part of the steel mill, the Rod and Wire Division. You could hear the work going on there.

Whila kind of snuggled against me in a way that invited me to put my arm up and around her shoulder. Her head leaned into my chest as if it were a pillow. Whila's perfume, which I learned later was called "White Shoulders," was strong.

She turned her body sideways to me, lifted her head up and offered me her lips. I bent down and kissed her, being careful to avoid bumping noses like Freda—kiss . . . soft . . . press . . . breathe . . . soft . . . pull back. I looked down at her eyes, which were closed, expecting a smile like Freda had given me.

Whila's eyelids snapped open and there was a faint smile, maybe a smirk, as if she was expecting more. "Can I have that again?" she breathed hoarsely.

As I bent down for another application of my best technique, her hand came up and laced itself in my hair, adding a gentle pressure on my head, so that at the peak of my kiss when I was slightly pressing her lips with mine—she gave me a flick, and then another, and then another, and then she let go, as she pulled back.

Time stood still for a moment as I considered what had just happened. I had heard of a French Kiss before, but no one I knew had ever done it—given or received. But there was no mistake about this. Whila had just transported me into another sphere and elevated me beyond all of my friends.

Whila wasn't finished. Her lips then pressed against my neck, kissing it—flick . . . flick . . . flick. I was tingling in places that had never tingled before. I'm sure I was covered with goose bumps from head to toe. She pulled back.

It wasn't over—there was more. Whila moved from my neck to my ear and simply breathed in my ear. This was unbelievable, the sensations that she was capable of provoking.

"Whila . . . time to come in," her mother called in a friendly way from the kitchen, but it was such a mood breaker that I kicked my legs straight out. When I did, though, I hit the banister and knocked both Coke bottles over into the bushes. I could have smashed the whole porch railing.

Jumping up on my feet in a flash, I straightened out my shirt. Whila had her hand over her mouth, giggling.

I started to laugh also, but it was a nervous laugh; Whila's laughter was because something was funny—me.

"Oh dear," she said. "You've got my lipstick all over your nice blue shirt."

A small price to pay for the revelations she had just bestowed. Then, reality caught up with me—I was going to have to face my mother and dad with lipstick on my shirt. I knew they would be waiting up for me when I got home at ten o'clock. Oh, Lord. What time is it? I looked at my Timex ("takes a licking and keeps on ticking")—eight-fifty.

"Don't worry about it. I'll stop at the gas station and wash it off," I said confidently, but without any idea of how I would do that. "Gosh, Whila, I had a really good time with you and I hope we can get together soon. Will I see you next week at the dance?"

"Well, you could come over sooner than that. Maybe after your paper route is finished?" she offered.

Paper route! Oh no. I left my paper bag, and my ring with everybody's stubs on it, and my paper punch in the locker at the Steelworkers Hall.

"Good idea. How about I stop over Monday, around five-thirty?" Something to look forward to. Whila came over to me, wrapped her arms around my waist, gave me a firm hug, and kissed me on the cheek.

"I'll see you Monday. Good night." She went inside the door, but our eyes never lost contact until I was beyond the next house.

What was I going to do about my paper route stuff and Whila's lipstick? I decided that there was nothing I could do about the paper route things tonight since the Steelworkers Hall closed at nine o'clock. I would have to go after it tomorrow morning. But the lipstick had to be dealt with. I walked to the center of town on Rhodes Avenue, avoiding Gallia where my paper route was, hoping that none of my customers would see me with Whila's lipstick on my shirt. I couldn't believe that I had gotten so distracted with the dance and with Whila that I would forget my paper route equipment.

Oh no. The lights at the Pure Oil gas station were out. I went closer and there was a sign in the window: "Closed for Death in Family. Will re-open Monday." I saw my reflection in the station's windows, and yes, there were lipstick smears on my shirt. Where could I go? Aha, the Pool Hall—the Tiger's Den. It was nine-fifteen. They were always open late.

I had never been in the pool hall at night. I had heard stories about what went on there—gambling, fights, women—so, I was a little nervous about going in, but the fear of having my mother see lipstick on me was stronger than my fear of the unknown. Upon entering the Tiger's Den, the place seemed dead. There was nobody behind the bar. Big Band music came softly from the jukebox while two guys played pool way in the rear of the place at the last table. Click. A ball ricocheted off another.

There was a restroom on the first floor, which I had used before, but it didn't have a mirror. Based on what others had said, the one downstairs not only had a mirror but also a shower—probably for those long days and nights of gambling at cards and pool, I guess. Downstairs was also the place that had the "bad reputation," where all the nasty stuff happened, but despite that, I started down the steps.

Quietly entering the mysterious basement area, I looked off to the left. A two-door doorway led to the back room. I saw men standing around a green, felt-covered card table. Some had their hands on their hips; others were looking down. All were hazed in cigarette smoke and overhead lights. A hushed conversation was going on, out of my sight.

It was dark where I was standing. Quietly, I walked to the bathroom that was off to my right. I opened the door and turned on the light, closing the door behind me. The room was a little larger and more highly decorated than I thought it would be. There was a padded bench to sit down on and three lockers against the opposite wall.

The washbasin was in a nice walnut cabinet with a shelf above it, and an oval mirror above that. On the shelf was a small wicker basket. Inside was a box of Gem double-edge razor blades, a box of Blue Star single-edge razor blades, two razors of each style, a styptic pencil, a pair of fingernail clippers and a bottle of Murine eye drops. Beside the small basket were bottles of St. John's Bay Rum and Old Spice after-shave lotion. Around the cabinet on the floor was a soft rubber mat to stand on, cushioning your feet. Next to the washbasin was the commode with a small horizontal window over it, and next to that was a shower. Between the commode and the shower was a little wooden shelf unit that held towels and washcloths. I locked the door with the only thing that seemed out of place—the lock was simply a hook that you put in a loop on the other side of the door. Now I was ready to begin.

I took a paper towel, wet it and rubbed soap on it. Then, looking in the mirror, I began rubbing the lipstick on my collar. After a minute of rubbing, I had lots of little bits of paper towel. I took the dry end of the paper towel and brushed away at the wet spot. The paper towel wasn't cutting it, so I took a washcloth and lathered it up. Much better. When I was finished, my collar was drenched but there was small evidence of any lipstick!

I repeated the process on my shirt pocket where Whila had laid her head (and her lips). The washcloth did the trick. The pocket was pretty wet, but not bad.

I hung the washcloth up, and just as I turned around to exit the bathroom, the door jiggled. A man's voice said, "Somebody in there? I'll come back."

Without thinking, I answered in my thirteen-year-old voice, "No, that's OK. I'm just leaving."

"Whaaat?" he said, as I opened the door.

"There you go." I said cheerfully with my wet blue shirt.

"Who the Sam Hill are you and what are you doing here in this bathroom?" the man said with an edge on his voice, as if I were in trouble.

I suddenly realized that I could have heard something that I shouldn't have heard, like what was going on in the other room. There didn't seem to be a good way out of this, me being a kid—even though my voice had changed.

I put on my most convincing voice and my most intelligent cadence. "Look, Sir, I'm Ron, the paperboy, and I deliver the newspaper here, and I was on my way home from the Friday Night Dance at the Steelworkers Hall, and I needed a bathroom with a mirror, so I came down here, and I'm sorry if I shouldn't have done that."

"Well, we'll see about that. Freddy's the night manager here—hey, Freddy—do you know this kid? He was in the bathroom just now. He says he's your paperboy."

"Naw," says Freddie, walking up, "never saw him before, but I don't start work here until way after the paper is delivered, so maybe he is. Why's your shirt wet in those places?" asked Freddie.

"Uuuuuuhhhhh," I cleverly gave myself time to sort through the record of the evening to see if anything would make sense—other than the truth. Two other men gathered around me. I couldn't find anything else to say, so I just went for it.

"Some girl kissed me and got her lipstick on my shirt and I had to get it off before I got home, because my mother would be mad," I offered.

Well, you would have thought that Jack Benny himself had told the funniest joke these men ever heard because they started howling. "Haaaa, haaa. OOOOh lipstick. Yoooowser. Haaaah. Haaah." They were elbowing each other.

One man said, "Well, kid, there's a lot worse places for that lipstick to have been other than on your collar. Your mom would really have had a lot of questions then."

And that set them off again. "Haaaa, haaa. OOOOh lipstick. Yoooowser. Haaaah. Haaah." I was embarrassed at being the butt of their laughter, but I couldn't do anything about it.

"Aw hell, kid, you're all right," as one of them put me in a friendly head-lock and squeezed, rubbing my hair, messing it up.

"You can come back anytime you got lipstick on ya, kid," said Freddie. "Just stop by and let us see where it is," and they went off again, "Haaaa, haaa. OOOOh lipstick. Yoooowser. Haaaah. Haaah."

I started walking up the stairs. "See ya, kid. Come on back sometime when ya can stay longer." And their laughter trailed away into Big Band music, as I emerged upstairs. Click. The pool game continued.

Outside the pool hall, I looked at my Timex—nine-forty. It was a seventeen-minute walk or a twelve-minute run to my house. I thought I would run. Starting at Cooper's Corner, off I went, running up Harrisonville Avenue past

... Pine Street
... Spruce Street
... Cedar Street
... Oak Street
... Maple Street
... Taft Street
... York Street

I slowed down. It was nine-fifty. I was a half block away from my house, so I knew I would be early, which was my goal—to prove that I was trustworthy.

I bounded up the steps, two at a time, opened the front screen door and walked in.

Dad was asleep on the couch. Mother was not. She was sitting in her chair watching TV. "Well, Ronald Dean, welcome home," she said. When my formal name was used, it generally meant that I was in trouble.

Mother chuckled, "It looks like you've had a time of it. Your hair's all messed up, you're sweating, and your shirt's got big wet spots on it." My turn to talk.

"Uuuhhh, well, I had a really nice time tonight," I affirmed.

"Anything, you want to tell me?" said Mother, in a voice tinged with suspicion—but also with encouragement.

"Well, now that you asked, there was this spaceship that landed on Gallia Street right outside the Steelworkers Hall and I thought about asking for a ride . . ." Mother interrupted me.

"All right, smarty pants. Why don't you have a glass of milk and some cookies, then clean yourself up, and go to bed."

She knew that something had happened but she chose not to pursue it. I hadn't been in a fight, I hadn't been smoking or drinking, and I was home early. I was thirteen and getting older every day, and she knew I was going to get into scrapes and have to get out of them on my own, so a little leeway here was a good thing.

"Thanks, Mother. Good night! . . . I love you." I was glad that my dad was asleep, because the questioning would have been more intense.

After washing up, I lay down in my bed and began reviewing the eventful day—dancing with Freda and Whila, losing my paper route stuff, lipstick on my shirt, the pool hall. Exhaustion took me to sleep before I could relive Whila's kiss.

The Girls Play Dress-Up

The dark one chooses the black gown, the fair one the white,
and both slip them on quickly, neither child having been given
permission to use them, and since the mother is occupied
elsewhere in the house, and their desire is overwhelming,
they take from her dresser drawers all that they need: a stole
shot with silver, a fox wrap, bracelets, gloves, pearls, and from
the bottom of the closet two pairs of heels which they put on
but do not walk in, each watching the other as she leans into
the glass to paint her lips and rouge her cheeks, each tasting
now the sour gall of envy, the dark one wanting to
wear the white gown, the fair one the black, and neither opening
her mouth to say so. It is the first day of the first June of the
Fifties, and all around them light is gilding the air, the kind of
flat and brassy end-of-the-evening midwestern light that comes
to them precisely like this just once and will not come again but
in the poverty of memory, a momentary luster playing itself out
in the mirror in which they can see only the other's face, what
each cannot help but covet, what they, though barely old enough
to name it, will both call beauty.

Pyrotechnicalities

Released from the humid geometry
of schoolrooms into summer's aimless drift,
from Diamond's blue box to a stolen
Zippo, we tested the incendiary properties
of cornstalks and sparrow wings,
of compact cow chips from neighbor Knapke's
pasture, and in those lengthened evenings
after supper when nothing sparked
imagination, stalked alleys buoyed
by burn barrels. And when abandoned barns
began to blaze that driest July on record,
we understood how blood quickens
to flame, how in those solemn
and curious gatherings at rural fences,
in that communal mass of bodies,
fire instructs ferocious camaraderie.
Still, after Knapke's barn ate itself
in one long breath one August night
and some village official spoke of mania,
seeing in the straw stockpiled inside
invitation enough, we put away
our fascination, and would have told
if anyone had thought to ask.

Painting Portsmouth

On a long northern stretch of the Ohio River shore there stands a 20-foot guard, its body concrete and its skin painted. It's a floodwall, built shortly after the overflowing river devastated the small town of Portsmouth, Ohio, in 1937. The city's protectorate hoped the wall would defend the town against the river's future uprisings. After the bare gray structure performed its duties admirably, deflecting two watery assaults in 1964 and 1997, Portsmouth's government honored it with a uniform. They commissioned an artist to paint the city's 2,000-year history on the floodwall's 2,000-foot canvas.

The murals are one of Portsmouth's few tourist attractions, longer than the dozen historic buildings and taller than the Native American mounds they depict. Not that the city attracts many travelers—the mural project was a palette of risk and hope. Steel and shoe industries had supported Portsmouth up until the 1980s, but after the plants shut down, so did the town; most people left for more promising prospects. But city officials were unwilling to drown the city's history, so they plastered it on the broadside of the floodwall, sweating hopes that it might bring some type of artsy revenue to Portsmouth's dilapidated skyline.

Artsy isn't the adjective most Portsmouth natives would use to describe their town, whose name they pronounce in singular style, dropping the fricative and softening the harsh s: Portshmif. Almost Southern with a touch of hillbilly, Portsmouthians serve up their words dripping with double negatives and rounded vowels. My first taste was when I brought my daughter to preschool: the teacher, large and round like the O she was about to pronounce, smiled broadly at us and asked, "Would you like to collar?" We looked blankly at her for a moment, until she held up some crayons and repeated her question. The slight southern lilt was endearing, although when my daughter came home weeks later saying phrases like, "I don't have no more," I decided to enforce a bit of northern grammar.

It must have been my strict New York accent that betrayed me to the natives: my hard o's and moratorium on *ain't* were blatant tipoffs. But when pronunciation wasn't enough, the local hamburger joint often took up the burden of announcing outsider origins. Like most buildings in Portsmouth, Hickie's is drooping on the corner of a run-down lot, with inadequate parking and a few barred windows. On our first pilgrimage to what the locals describe as the mecca of burger joints, my husband and I waited in line inconspicuously, examining the framed fames—pictures of high school football teams mostly—preserved in photograph and hung on the chipping red painted wall.

"What'll ya have?" the cashier asked when we turned to the counter. We had just started asking what came on the hamburgers when she interrupted us with a smile. "You ain't never been here before! Hey guys," she said, turning to the cooks and waitresses directly behind her, "we got us some virgins!" Apparently this was a reason to celebrate, so they gave us an honorary chorus of *Hickie's Virgin*—a reputation-smearing call-out to publicize the fact that we were virgin customers, virgin authentic burger-eaters, and (obviously) virgin Portsmouthians. We lost our innocence pretty quickly after that.

Hickie's has been part of the Portsmouth landscape for over three decades. It was built during Portsmouth's industrial boom, a prosperous span of years that is captured in memorial detail on the floodwall murals. On one section is a still life of an old steel plant with a gargantuan bucket suspended by iron hangers, pouring fire from its gray belly into the open maw of a vat. In another, there is a long parade of shoes on a belt, with an assembly line of workers hurrying like mothers to tie laces. But the mural frames read like gravestones: *Steel Production, 1870–1980; Shoe Manufacturing, 1869–1977*. By 1981, the smoke from the industrial boom had dissipated. Steel shops closed, shoe factories went out of business, and over fifteen thousand people left the town to follow the money, leaving the population at half what it once was. And with the fall of the major industries came unemployment; with unemployment came increased drug use; and with increased drug use came death.

There's another mural in Portsmouth, one that doesn't celebrate, but mourns. On a large department store window, members of SOLACE have posted pictures and names of deceased family members. Most of the deceased were victims of prescription drug abuse, a plague that has swept over Portsmouth in the last twenty years. The drug epidemic is so widespread, the courts and hospital so overwhelmed, that many see it as another type of devastating flood—another mural dedicated to remembering what was.

When I brought up the drug problem to my freshman writing class at Shawnee State, there were the common responses, the obligatory, "I gotta get out of this town," so frequently embraced by townies, but there were other sentiments too. One girl, with bright brown eyes, a big smile, and typical Portsmouth friendliness, spoke somewhat fiercely: "The drugs haven't won yet, though. I mean, yeah, they're everywhere, but there're still people in town who want this place to be what it was."

"And what was it?" I asked.

This time another student spoke up—a guy in a sweatshirt with the hood shadowing his eyes. "It's a hometown," he said. "People here care about the right stuff."

A few years ago, "the right stuff" was an eight-ton sandstone boulder buried in the Ohio River, known as Indian Head Rock. The rock is mystical history at its best: enigmatic carvings have been etched all over its surface, from a cartoonish face to runic letters. A century ago, the rock used to peek out just above the surface of the water, but after the damming of the river in the '20s, Indian Head Rock was flooded over and immersed. In 2008, Steve Shaffer, a passionate historian from nearby Portsmouth, decided to salvage the rock so that its unique history could be enjoyed by more than just fish. After lifting it from the river, he turned it over to the mayor of Portsmouth, who couldn't have been more pleased.

Kentucky, however, separated from Portsmouth by only a tall white bridge, was furious. They claimed the rock had been in Kentucky waters, that it had been stolen; Ohio retaliated, declaring that it was on their side of the line. The debate was fought over in federal court, and for the first time ever, Portsmouth made national headlines. In the end, Kentucky won. The courts said that the rock really was within Kentucky boundaries. But what I think really happened was a Solomon solution: someone offered to cut the rock in half, and Portsmouth officials, defenders of history, let it go.

Although history paints the town with colorful anecdotes, the story of Portsmouth isn't in its past, but in its people. My husband and I arrived in Portsmouth with an overstuffed twenty-six-foot truck, with only ourselves and our three small children to help unpack. As we snapped a picture of the SOLD sign on the front yard, our two neighbors walked over, welcomed us to the neighborhood, and asked if they could help us unload. For the next two hours, they hauled in chairs, tables, toys, dressers, all the mess we'd gathered from living all over the U.S.—Utah, Iowa, New York, Idaho—and placed it slowly in our new house. On the east coast, in the mountainous west, even on the windy plains of Iowa, no neighbor had ever made a town become home so quickly.

Weeks later I visited the local farmer's market, stopping by the corn stand to choose a few bright yellow ears. An older lady, dressed in Bermuda shorts and a pink-striped shirt, was shucking her corn into the large trash can. "Hot summer, isn't it?" she asked conversationally as I paused to strip the cobs.

"Sure is." (I was learning to tone down my more formal phrases by this point).

"My husband can't stand no heat," she went on. "He likes to stay inside 'til the evenin' weather."

"Sounds like a good idea to me!"

She smiled. "Unless of course he has to mow the lawn," she announced cheerfully. "Funny thing 'bout husbands, isn't it? They'll do whatever they gotta to keep the lawn lookin' good, but for themselves it's always grubby T-shirts!" By the time the corn was clean, I knew more about the peculiarities of husbands than I had learned in my seven years of marriage. In New York we might have labeled this crazy, but only because we weren't familiar with the phrase "southern hospitality." And that's what makes Portsmouth endure.

There's one section of the murals that epitomizes Portsmouth, both its history and its people. It's an image of the 1937 flood, a collage of captured moments of the flood's wake. A lonely boat floats on water twenty feet above street level; the long line of the downcast homeless waits at the soup kitchen; people with vacant, cheerless eyes stand on rooftops and wait for rescuers. The whole section is done in shades of gray: gray waters, gray people, gray skies, gray boats. On the right side there's gray, foreboding, turbulent water, and melting into the waves is a woman, a cry frozen on her face, and in her outstretched arms she's holding a child above the rioting water. A man in a nearby boat reaches out, grasping the child's small hand—

The mural pauses there, the moment petrified in paint, but the story continues on a gravestone in Portsmouth City Cemetery. Bessie Tomlin, a young pregnant mother, held her toddler above waters until a rescue boat finally reached them. As a fireman pulled the child to safety, Bessie sank beneath the waves.

The floodwaters took her, just as the river submerged Indian Head Rock and the waves of drug abuse threatened Portsmouth. On the day I moved away, I looked back as I crossed the white bridge over the Ohio River. I could see the south side of the wall, its silvery-gray face glinting in the sun like a shield. Portsmouth was surrounded by guardians: a floodwall to keep watch over the river, murals to preserve the past, and people who make the town endure. It's the people who make Portsmouth more than just a picture on a wall, more than just history. They make it a home.

Kathleen's Talent

I have come to this town with my mother's old kitchen sifter to diligently screen
    the air, earth
and water, to observe the small implements, the leavings, the bones, the mental
    shards that can
be found in the rare moments of Portsmouth, Ohio. With my new polished trowel
    I shall scrape
the skin and texture of this city to see if I cannot unearth the mysterious fire, that
    unerring
tessitura which seems to scale the air like the German Wallendas who with sure
    balance walked the
perils of the air, unafraid. In my type of work you are never sure of what you will
    find. You may,
ultimately, come up empty handed. Still, I think, some element of Kathleen's
    special sound is
somewhere engendered in the walls of the town, or somewhere permeating the
    obscure alleys
where no single citizen travels any longer. The origins of such a talent is, I think,
    buried possibly,
in the earth or resting in desperation, in the mind of some old, early ancient voice
    teacher who,
defying the odds of intention sought to extend and preserve the art of singing in
    this esophagus. I
have come to delve into the creation of this town's well-kept wealth. Perhaps the
    answer is not to
be found in the wanting of some citizen inadvertently uttering a local truth they
    deem to be only
theirs. It may be in the random fear that no one wants to be found wanting. I am
    here to mine the
specific essence of that special human voice as it scales the mountainous trees, and
    glides further
into those regions of autumnal hollows where even the sky appears transcendent
    in the echoes of
pure pitch gliding through the human heart.

Route 4

Take it
from Dayton through corn
and soybeans to Lake Erie,
eat maple nut ice cream
from Woody's and watch
the barns drift by.
Wave to the people
lolling in porch swings
and they'll wave back.
Take your time—
stop for LIVE BAIT and fish Honey Creek,
have dinner at Bubbles Burgers,
then see a play
at the Attica Little Theatre.

Ask for directions at a gas station
and three bystanders
will help the attendant
tell you the way
to Milford Center, Marion,
Bucyrus, Chatfield, or Reedtown.
They'll all wish you a safe trip
and someone will say
Hurry back, now.

The best place to stay
is the Stay Inn,
and the best breakfast
is at the Hen House,
where you'll want to take a biscuit crust
and sop up the last of the sausage gravy.

Next door you can pick out a Bible
in purple leather for Aunt Gladys
from J & R's Gospel Gift Shop.

The welcome sign assures you that
Salvation Is All You Need
at the Mechanicsburg
Church of God,
whose fallen parishioners
lie a few steps from the door
with all the time in the world.

Portrait of Southern Ohio in 5-Syllable Road Signs

Woodchipper for Rent
Danger! Rocks Below!
Registered Holsteins
Adopt a Highway
Pres. Harding's Birthplace
Progressive Euchre
Troubled? Try Praying.
Soccer Conference Champs
Long Live Rock & Roll
Ceramic Lawn Pets
New Development
Re-elect John Glenn
The County's Best Yarn
Slippery When Wet
Sarah We Miss You
Hardy Mums for Sale
Private Property
Forget the Damned Dog—
    Beware of Owner!
Electric Co-Op
Next Stop Defiance
WalMart Coming Soon

In This Reality, You Exit at the Next McDonald's for Fries and a Shake

Somewhere in some alternate universe, there's a reality where you do get off at the next exit just to photograph the red barn. You're not a professional, but why should you let that stop you from taking a good, artsy picture now and then? Who knows, maybe you're an outsider artist and don't even know it? And even the professionals have to start somewhere. If you don't end up with a picture you can sell, at least you'll have something to show friends when they're over the house getting tanked on margaritas. It's a pleasant thing to show someone a photograph you took yourself. You watch the lines on her face soften. A smile blooms. She looks from the photo to you, then back to the photo, and you can see in her eyes that you're somehow more than you were before.

You Just Sit There Dreaming

It's about all I can take. A seagull walks across a Wal-Mart lot,
so far inland. Yet when the gull calls, waves crash in after.
If you're listening hard. If you're leaning out with both hands
cupped at your ear shells, almost falling off your bench.
Anything to get away from this town, this blank spot between two exits.
What they really need to sell in there is wings, you'd say
to whoever was sitting beside you if anyone was sitting beside you.
A full feather suit and a map to get away. Momentarily distracted,
smiling, you close your eyes, lean back and dream of opening a box.
The wind from a seagull's wings, even from so far above,
rustles both your eyebrows as it beats away without you.

The Fair

As a child, the only time I ever missed the Ohio State Fair was when I had pneumonia at eight or nine. *Who gets pneumonia in the summer?* I wondered that year, tossing and turning on Grandma Jan's floral couch, my fever making me wiggle like a loose tooth. It was one of the last summers before Dad married Julie. Dad eventually started taking me alone to the fair because of the uncanny way my stepmom had of making me feel invisible. I hated the way she picked even the most microscopic pieces of onion out of anything: Julie had the palate, and the temperament, of a preschooler. When Dad met her (he was forty-one, she was twenty-five), Mom kidded him mercilessly. "What do you do together, Kent?" she'd ask. "Take her out for Happy Meals? Tell her to save the toys for Hayley."

The first time I couldn't make it to the State Fair as an adult was during my summer-long solo road trip to Canada in 2008. I remember feeling incredibly nostalgic for the butter cow and the giant slide when I was in Québec, wishing I could share the silly annual midwestern tradition with the British boy I'd found on my travels and with whom I'd inconveniently fallen in love. For as much as I missed the fair that summer, I've only been back once since then, and I find myself missing Dad's perennial question: "Are we getting wristbands for the rides this year?" he always asked, trying to save a few bucks on unlimited passes for rides instead of paying for each one individually. After all, you never know when you'll find a rare presidential campaign button or vintage license plate in the commercial building.

"No, not this time, Dad," I'd always answer. "Just the Ferris wheel." I never did like the rides much, as I always got nauseous on the ones where you can hear people screaming from fifty feet in the air. In my mind, the fair was never about the rides, or even the midway, really, though I won a few stuffed animals over the years, and a host of inflatable toys: several baseball bats, one Reds bat staying displayed in my bedroom long enough that it taught me to spell "Cincinnati"; an enormous hammer I could use to bonk my friends on the head; and my very favorite, a hot pink electric guitar. I had a fascination with inflatables, as I called them, when I was a kid, and I wonder what ever happened to the ones that sat next to me in the backseat as I slept during the long drive home from Columbus every year. Maybe I'd even put the little pink guitar next to Lola, my real guitar, that's on display next to my fireplace.

Since it's not the midway, with its flashing cheap neon lights and throngs of teenagers, that makes the fair so special for me, what is it? Dad and I are traditionalists by nature. For us, the fair is about cramming sunscreen, cameras, chapstick, tickets, and a map inside a fanny pack. Going down the giant slide five times on those old burlap sacks; laughing at Dad's stories about going down it as a teenager in formations with his friends, like synchronized swimmers. Being lobster red and freckled by noon despite copious amounts of SPF 100. Watching carefully for cow patties and wiping your shoes on the grass at least a dozen times before putting a toe on Grandma Jan's white carpet. Having your T-shirt stained pink from a dripping ice cream cone, or when your shins and tennis shoes are sticky with chocolate for hours. Carrying around a blue Icee half as big as you are and taking bets on whether Dor-Lo pizza will be there that year or not. Rushing to see what or who they've decided to sculpt out of butter this year in addition to the perennially appearing Butter Cow. Having to buy a sweatshirt in the commercial building because it dropped to 40° in August, or putting a chilled pop bottle on the back of your neck to relieve the heat. The fair is about the sore muscles you always have the next day, and the excitement over breaking a new record: *12 straight hours at the fair; 13; 15½.*

For us, the fair is about the picture we take next to the giant cement cardinal near the fairground's entrance. I can trace my childhood through those cardinal pictures, because as much as the overgrown Ohio state bird stayed the same, I changed, and Dad changed, with startling regularity.

*

The northern cardinal, *Cardinalis cardinalis*, was once prized as a songbird because of its distinctive calls and vibrant red plumage. One can imagine that the bird was popular, too, because of the little black face mask that's prominent in the male, but a faded gray-brown, like her feathers, in the female. The longest-living cardinal in captivity is recorded to have made it to the ripe old age of twenty-eight, while the oldest wild cardinal that we know of lived to be only fifteen. Cardinals mate for life, and the primary function of its song is to protect its turf and to locate its partner: when the bird is in immediate danger, its calls become louder and more assertive, culminating in a series of short, metallic chirps. Nested pairs often travel together, and the cardinal can be found from southern Canada to certain regions of Mexico, from the eastern seaboard to West Texas. Since the Migratory Bird Treaty Act of 1918, the sale of the bird has been illegal, and now the cardinal is, instead, the mascot of two professional and eleven college sports teams.

The northern cardinal is the state bird of seven states, more than any other bird. It was almost the state bird of Delaware, too, until the state decided to opt instead for the gas flame–blue plumage of the Blue Hen of Delaware. I wonder now if other states have the carnation as their state flower, or tomato juice—chosen as Ohio's beverage in 1965—as their state drink of choice, because I was always under the impression that each state had its own bird. For some reason, I thought each one had to be unique.

Cardinals aren't very migratory birds; instead, they take up permanent residence near where they were born. If the weather's bad enough or there's no food, they'll leave, but it's not routine. Once the nesting pair stakes a claim, they stay put, defending their territory until the last. Cardinals don't need to move. They're content with where they are.

*

I have this thing about going on drives.

More often than not, these drives are a distraction, a way to waste time, an intentional delaying of deadlines, due dates, and responsibility. They're usually accidental—the trip to the grocery to pick up milk or paper towels turning into a two-hour-long excursion because of the way the late afternoon light cascades through the leaves of the sweet gum tree outside my apartment, the breeze cool, the sun hot—but occasionally, because I can feel in my tissues that I need them, I set out to get lost on purpose. My bodily craving for movement is like a sodium deficiency or when the doctor says you're low on B12, and my desire to wander has metastasized other, competing desires: to stay, to settle down, to be at peace; to have kids, a spouse, a savings account. And so I drive, racking up the miles and learning the back roads like the back of my hand, never quite knowing where I am or when, if ever, I'll finally be able to be happy while standing still.

EVERY RIVER ON EARTH

When I went on that two-month-long solo road trip at twenty-two, across New England and eastern Canada, I asked my closest friends to make CDs for me, a homemade soundtrack for adventures they, and I, never could have predicted. Dad was the only family member to make recommendations, though they took the form of a list since I'm not sure he'd even know how to burn a CD. The list was full of 70s classics, America's "Sister Golden Hair" and "Ventura Highway," which he claims is the greatest road trip song of all time. Missing from the list, though, was what Dad sang me as a lullaby, James Taylor's "Sweet Baby James." It is what my cell phone plays when he calls; it's what will play at my wedding—when or if I have it—for our father and daughter dance.

I don't actually remember Dad ever singing me this song. I only know he did from Mom's stories, her hazy recollections of the frigid winter nights twenty-five years ago when I was brought home, swaddled and secure. I can hardly picture Dad singing at all, except for when he'd make up silly songs to get a laugh or do Jimmy Buffett impersonations. Regardless, I am nostalgic for the memory of this lullaby, in all its implications: that I was once a small, blank slate; that there was a time before he moved away.

*

As a toddler, I liked to run away from my parents. I started crawling out of my crib when I was a year old, I'd pull myself up and over the top of my playpen, and I even learned how to wiggle out of my high chair. Dad had to install extra straps and buckles just so he and Mom could feed me jarred peas and apricots without me leaping off the plastic tray. "You weren't like other kids," Mom tells me whenever I call to ask her about my childhood antics. They tried everything, harnesses, leashes, and even extra locks on the screen door after I managed to get outside and lock my mom out of the house when I was three. Dad took me to an annual crafts festival in Metamora, Indiana, one year, and when he wasn't looking, I squirmed out of my stroller, running headlong into the crowd of twenty thousand. The way he tells it, Dad took off running after me, dragging the stroller behind him, and yelling for people to clear the way. He caught me eventually, and I imagine I would've just laughed and giggled at his red face and the beads of sweat on his forehead when he finally scooped me up in his arms. *What a fun game*, I might've thought; *he chased me!* I'm struck now by the fact that

I don't call Dad for research, in my compulsion to be as faithful to my own truth as I can be. Instead, I just tell him, warn him, that he's in my writing, and that no, his appearances aren't particularly unflattering. Why don't I call, why don't I wonder how far he'd follow me now?

By the time of my earliest memory of the Ohio State Fair, Mom and Dad had figured out that they needed to physically tie me into the stroller if they didn't want to lose me in the swarm of people for good. I remember lying on my back and staring up into an overcast sky and at the looming shadows of my parents, and trying to free my chubby arms and legs. Suddenly, I saw an enormous figure standing several stories tall, or so it had seemed from my toddler perspective: it was an inflatable Wendy, the mascot from Wendy's, the fast-food chain founded in Dublin, Ohio, a town not far from Columbus and known for its annual Celtic Festival. Her iconic pigtails stuck out from the sides of her head like bright red antennae, and her robin egg blue eyes were wide, like the quizzical expression of my Cabbage Patch dolls. I remember feeling terrified at the sheer size of her, and at how she kept smiling as she rocked gently in the wind, her hands lifeless at her sides. It was when I realized that she, too, was tethered, kept in place by ropes and stakes, that I felt less afraid. She was, perhaps, a kindred spirit, and I could picture both of us floating up and up and up until we were tiny flecks of color on the horizon.

*

Most of the world's countries have a national bird: Antigua claims the magnificent frigatebird, *Fregata magnificens,* an all-black bird with a brilliant red throat pouch that has been known to travel over four thousand miles from its breeding grounds. The Bahamas gets the Caribbean flamingo, *Phoenicopterus ruber,* those walking, living lawn ornaments I've loved since I was a child and my dad decorated my bedroom in vintage flamingo bric-a-brac: a ceramic planter, a picture frame, plastic shot glasses from Florida. Belize chose *Ramphastos sulfuratus,* the toucan of so much American breakfast cereal fame; Jamaica's choice, *Trochilus polytmus,* or the doctor bird, matches the colors of the country's flag, the bird's breast neon yellowish green against stark black wings. Each of the eleven Canadian provinces has an official bird—from Newfoundland's Atlantic puffin to the Northwest Territory's gryfalcon to Québec's snowy owl—but Canada has no national bird, no eagle with an olive branch in its talons on currency and commemorative china. Some of the birds stay only in the countries that have claimed them, never seeing anything beyond the borders of Mexico or Montenegro. Others fly far and fast from where they're born, only to come back when they're ready to lay eggs of their own. Some never do come back.

I remember Dad taking me to the Cincinnati Zoo when I was a kid. Between all the fun animals—the big cats, the penguins, the elephants—he always made a point to stop by the Passenger Pigeon memorial. Martha, the last existing specimen of *Ectopistes migratorius*, died at the zoo in 1914, despite the fact that up until the latter half of the nineteenth century, flocks of passenger pigeons would often be hundreds of miles long. The pigeons could fly as fast as highway traffic, and would sometimes not return to a place for years, choosing to instead go in new directions. After all, the word "migratory" is in the bird's name. Once people figured out that passenger pigeon meat was cheap food for slaves and servants, hunters would kill tens of thousands of birds at a time, snatching entire flocks out of the air and into nets. "What happened to them, Dad?" I'd ask as I studied Martha's lifeless taxidermic frame. I wasn't yet aware that something could cease to exist outside of photographs, paintings, and museum-mounted skeletons. That something could suddenly leave and not come back.

"They're extinct," he said. "They're all gone."

*

Despite the Ohio State Fairgrounds' Natural Resources area's games of archery and fishing, to me, that part of the grounds always had a serious air to it. This is perhaps because of the myriad displays on boating safety, statistics about how many people drown in Ohio each year, and pamphlets warning against wildfire. I learned early, from the pamphlets and the park rangers, that nature is both beautiful and cruel, and that it is dangerous both to run free and to be trapped in pens and houses. On my last visit to the fair, we saw a coyote so sick of chain-link, so anxious and insane, that he wouldn't deviate from circling around a well-worn figure-eight pattern in his cage, not even pausing to rest or take a drink of stagnant fake pond water. He walked so fast around the tiny space that he was almost a scraggly gray-brown blur, and the ground beneath his feet was noticeably lower than in the rest of the enclosure, a tiny dust cloud arising with each harried step. As I stood and watched him, Dad having already moved on to marvel at the bald eagle or the falcons, the coyote stopped, panting slightly, and stared at me, his eyes haunted, hollow. I don't know what made him veer from his course, but that creature—meant to hunt, skulk, and scavenge through the shadows—seemed to find comfort and sanity in the thousands of laps around his cage. Even though he was fed and safe from predators and cars, he had to run. Perhaps the running is what kept him alive; maybe stopping to lie down in the shade would have killed him.

I was told recently by a colleague, one I have great respect for, that I "need a crisis." This was an observation that, once articulated, seemed a kind of revelation. *Who knew others could see and recognize that part of me?* It's something I've always known to be true about myself—a thought that's woken me in a cold sweat, one confided to friends in hushed telephone calls—but I'm not sure what it says about me that I'm impelled to inject chaos into my own life in order to create. We like to fool ourselves into believing that we're different, special, strange. Is that all I'm doing, but on a grand scale? What if I'm just trying to convince myself that I'm not exactly like everybody else?

What if I *am* exactly like everybody else?

*

Some kids are afraid of Santa Claus. They cry at the thought of climbing onto his lap and facing his stubble and fake beard; they run and hide at the mere thought of the red suit and the white fur collar, the grubby department store elves. Other children are scared of the Easter bunny, that overgrown, silent, smiling garden pest, and refuse both chocolate and bribes so they can avoid his touch. There are those who cover their ears, put their heads down, and cry during the entire fireworks display on the Fourth of July, the rapid-fire cannon sounds vibrating too viscerally through their little bones. Kids are scared of lots of things. As a little girl, I swam freely in the deep end of the pool, in the ocean, and in Lake Cumberland. I talked to strangers. I rode horses and even a rollercoaster or two, before I decided never to step foot on one again. So what was I afraid of as a kid? Smokey the Bear and Zambora the Gorilla Girl, both found at the fair.

Smokey's a somewhat friendly figure in his warnings against loose matches and campfires, but the Smokey at the State Fair is two stories tall and animatronic. As if that weren't enough for a kindergartner to be afraid of, he somehow—and this was one of the great mysteries of my childhood, like how the tooth fairy got money under my pillow without waking me—always knew my name. I remember standing in the wooded Natural Resources pavilion where Smokey is stationed with other kids my age. Looking around at all the bewildered faces, I felt nervous, anxious, ready to be punished. He was just so big in the eyes of a five-year-old, and it didn't matter that I couldn't yet work a book of matches and that I wasn't even allowed to be in the same room as an open flame. Somehow, I was the one responsible for wildfires and the destruction of the country's natural resources. After parents retrieved their cameras from their fanny packs and purses, Smokey's vacant stare would sweep over the crowd, and suddenly, a voice would boom down from the heavens: "Have you been a good girl, Hayley?" Smokey asked in a deep, congenial tone. "Are you doing your part to prevent forest fires?" You'd think that, to a five-year-old, a giant talking teddy bear with a felt hat, who knew your name, would be the best thing in the world, but it took me five, maybe six years to want to see Smokey again, and even longer than that to figure out the secret: while the kids weren't looking, one of the rangers walked around with a pen and notepad, collecting names. The man who supplied Smokey with a voice (thinking of him now reminds me a bit of the wizard behind the curtain in *The Wizard of Oz*) would then read them, giving the parents a once-in-a-lifetime photo op to capture their children's expressions of joy or, in my case, shock.

At least Smokey the Bear meant well. Zambora the Gorilla Girl was all about fear, like the Tower of Terror at Disney World, the 100 mph speeds of breakneck rollercoasters, or scare-the-pants-off-you movies like *Paranormal Activity* or even *The Blair Witch Project*, which was terrifying to me when I watched it, alone, at twelve. The whole sideshow was enclosed inside a tent—a brilliant marketing strategy that made Zambora as mysterious as a UFO and as compelling as a train wreck—with hand-painted scenes from Zambora's awful transformation from mild-mannered girl to hideous ape, the lost link in the evolutionary chain. I was only convinced to undertake the Zambora experience once, and I never even ended up seeing her. It was the first year Julie came with us, I think, before she and Dad married. I would've been eight, and the fearlessness of my first few years was already wearing off—I didn't ride rollercoasters anymore, and things like bugs and heights and death made me antsy, nervous. "Do you want to see her this year, Hayley?" Dad asked, like he did every year. I'd always said no, but I wanted to impress this leggy blonde woman who addressed my father in baby talk and who sometimes spent the night.

"Okay," I said, nodding, putting on the performance of appearing puffed up and brave, something I still do.

The inside of the tent was black, dark even after my eyes adjusted from the bright August sunlight. A disembodied voice repeated, looping the same phrases again and again, "Warning! If you have a weak heart, are an expectant mother, or are easily frightened, do not experience Zambora!" *I'm easily frightened!* I remember thinking. *What if I pass out or something?* The tent was packed, and I stood between Dad and Julie, the crowd jostling us back and forth against shoulders, elbows, and purses. I saw a single spotlight appear at the front of the tent, but because of the thicket of teenagers and slightly sadistic parents, I didn't know who, if anyone, was standing on the stage. Someone, or just the recording again, I couldn't tell, began speaking: "The Gorilla Woman will be locked in a solid steel cage for your protection. Under the bright lights you'll see the change begin. . . ." Dad and Julie exchanged grins and knowing glances as we were told about the scientific miracle we were to witness: the brow becoming heavier and more pronounced; the eyes growing dark, dilated, and angry; fangs appearing in a flash of yellowed enamel; dense black fur spreading over the body like moss. My pulse quickened. My palms were slick with sweat. My tongue was dry and my legs were weak, and I couldn't even see a thing. "The steel bars," the voice said, "they can't hold her anymore. Zambora's breaking loose!"

That's all I needed to hear to spur my quick exit. I elbowed past Dad, tore through the crowd, and fumbled for the tent opening in a panic. The blinding light of the outside was a relief, and I looked around: the ride with the spinning strawberries was still there, and so was the lemon shake-up stand. The Ferris wheel was still turning, and in the distance, I heard the All-Ohio State Fair Youth Band playing one of their afternoon shows. I felt some relief knowing that the world outside Zambora's tent had kept on going, but the relief was accompanied by the weight of embarrassment. *I'm a coward*, I thought. Only minutes after I came fumbling out of Zambora's tent, I heard a huge, collective scream, and then everyone ran out at once. I stood there, sheepish, my hands crossed in front of me as I waited for my dad and Julie to come and claim me.

Not unlike the indelible impression my stepmother's cruelty made on me, even though Zambora has been gone for years now, recalling the physical terror I felt at the sideshow's sleight-of-hand to this day invokes the stuff of nightmares. Dad still teases me about that summer. It never was about Zambora, though, not really. It was instead about looking like a coward, of giving in to flight rather than fight, about Julie seeing me bested by a cheap circus trick. "If you're easily frightened, do not experience Zambora!" the recording reiterates within my memory. "Want to see the gorilla woman this year, Hayley?" Dad will sometimes ask, grinning. I'm not sure if I'd go to see her even now.

Looking back, I see I sometimes was a nervous child, but what I don't understand is how I got that way. What made me shift from the fearless, Houdini-like little girl I was—always looking for a way to escape strollers, high chairs, tethers and constraints—into the uneasy, self-conscious teenager I would become? At twenty-six, I can still remember the churning sadness and anger in my stomach brought on by Julie ignoring me, not letting me hold my own half-brothers as babies, or calling me "princess" behind my back. The way she asked Dad to tell me not to hum at the dinner table. She always made fun of him for loving music, for the fact that he played clarinet and was the drum major of his high school marching band. One of Dad's very favorite things about the fair is the Ohio All-State Band, especially when they play his all-time favorite piece of music, John Philip Sousa's "Stars and Stripes Forever." Dad, who's been to the fair almost every year of his life, loves to tell a story about when he played clarinet in the Brookhaven High School marching band and attended a ceremony, led by former governor James A. Rhodes, where buckeye trees were planted at the fairground in 1969. The marching band played "Stars and Stripes Forever" then, and the State Fair band plays it now—we like to critique it every year, picking apart the piccolo soloist's every note. Julie, though, called dad a "nerd" and a "geek" for doing so, and by asking me to stop my humming, she tried her best to quash my need to sing. I've learned, though, that my song is vital: it is not only my way of calling out in joy or sadness, but also one of the best ways I have of overcoming fear.

*

I sometimes wonder how I'll ever have the courage to leave the Midwest, the place I love and that gave me birth, but that I've known I had to run from since I knew what running was. There's a saying in Ohio that, if it's a good growing season, corn should be "knee-high by the Fourth of July." Unlike the long haul to the cabin in Kentucky, with acre after acre of tobacco and the wide leaves hanging to dry, brittle and brown, in barns, the two-and-a-half hours on I-70 to the State Fair or to my grandparents' house in Columbus was nothing but corn. I probably learned the saying from Dad, though I can't say when, since it's so long been a part of the way I conceptualize Ohio, my home, with its rich, black soil and flat horizons. It never occurred to me that the saying wasn't universal, that corn grows at other rates in other places and sometimes, not at all. In the Carolinas, for example, farmers plant and cultivate almost a month before we do, and so their corn, on a good year, might be waist- or even shoulder-high under the kaleidoscope of July fireworks. In New England, the late frosts and strong sea breezes put crops at risk early in the season, and so the corn might not even be tasseling—that is, beginning to grow the silk cursed by kids roped into husking it on front porches and cement steps—by July.

It's easy, I think, to see the places we go and the people who live there through the lens of our own experience. We go through our days with blinders on, expecting that everyone sees the world the way we see it, grows the same crops, eats the same things, believes the same things. When we go to the Eiffel Tower, the Coliseum, or to kiss the Blarney Stone, we wear jean shorts, ball caps, sunscreen, and a money belt, scramble for T-shirts, paperweights, refrigerator magnets. We buy the guidebook; we don't speak to strangers; we worry; we are as afraid as skittish horses. This would seem, on the surface, an asinine way to travel. Why get a passport and shell out thousands of dollars to behave in other places the way we do at home? Why leave our homes at all? And yet it's comforting in our little bubble, our tiny corner of the globe, soothing in its familiarity. There's a reason why no summer feels complete for me without the State Fair, why I felt nostalgic for it that summer in Québec even though Dad and I have been twenty-three times, following the same itinerary every time. My experience of the fair—unique in that I hate the rides and love the Bahama Mama sandwiches from Schmidt's, look forward to the ugly cakes competition, speed past the midway, and take pictures posing with the Butter Cow—is woven into what summer means to me. Even though, over the years, we've brought my best friend, two boyfriends, and an ex-stepmother with us on our pilgrimage, Dad's a fixture at the fair. A given. An irreplaceable part of the equation. A universal.

*

In this photo next to the cement cardinal, I am twenty-four. It's the perfect kind of day for the fair: the sky blue as the blue Icee I'd have later; the sun directly above us, noon sun, maybe; the fuchsia and periwinkle petunias open and full in the background. Behind us, there's a souvenir stand with the inflatable figures of Dora the Explorer and SpongeBob SquarePants secured by clothespins in neat rows, their rounded sides gleaming in the sun. There are signs for ATMs and a Jeep dealership; there's the small tent, too, where Dad buys his State Fair pins. It's July, the day after we've returned from the stoic, rolling hills of Gettysburg and Antietam, the stone wall and the Burnside Bridge, and I'm still shell-shocked. After all our years of talking about it, we'd finally gone together. After watching Dad's Civil War sabers, rifles, canteens, and kepis move from apartment to house to house, writing reports, and watching Ken Burns documentaries, we finally did it.

It's not a bad cardinal picture, but I have a terrible sunburn from clavicle to cleavage, and I remember that it stung for days afterward. I'm not at my thinnest since my gastric bypass, but I look healthy. Happy. I know this because I'm smiling with my mouth open, teeth and all. Dad smiles with his mouth closed; thinking about it, I don't know if I could name a single photo where he smiles wide, a truly candid picture. I'm taller than he is, as I have been since I was nine or ten—I usually avoid heels around Dad, and sometimes purposely slouch a little. Here, I wear Chuck Taylors. Dad wears a Panama Jack T-shirt that's almost entirely plain on the front, with large, colorful graphics on the back. I think he's always liked T-shirts like that, with art on the back—Jimmy Buffett "Margaritaville" ones with parakeets and rum; L.L. Bean ones with moose or snowshoes—because they make him appear young and up-to-date. Cool. He got rid of the customary fanny pack years ago for precisely that reason. "That's so not-cool, Dad," I said. "Only dorks wear fanny packs."

With each cardinal picture, I tend to seem taller, slimmer, and have longer hair. Dad gets more handsome, I think, because I vastly prefer his beard over the immaculate mustache he kept for thirty years. He's a bit more paunchy these days, but still with strong, muscular legs: hiking legs, Cub Scout leader legs. Even though when I was a little girl, people thought I was the spitting image of my mother, I look more and more like Dad every year. We've both got oversized Van Houten noses, named for the slightly hooked noses (Mom calls it a "Roman nose") that characterize Grandma Jan's side of the family. It's a nose that demands attention, respect. A cubic zirconium stud, in my case. And there's the "Hughes Hair" as my cousin Anne calls it, the coarse, incredibly thick black hair that makes everyone think I'm Jewish, Greek, Italian, or Gypsy. "German," I tell them. "And some Irish, French, and a whole lot of Kentucky." We're a pair, all right: Dad and I are two people who, no matter what, will never agree on much, will remain stubborn, wry, and unable to ever quite persuade the other, and we will always follow precisely the same script when we say good-bye on the phone. It's like when I was a little girl and he still tucked me in at night: "You're the cutest and the sweetest," he'd say every night as he began to close the door. "And you're the most handsome and debonair," I'd reply. Even though I didn't really know what "debonair" meant, it wasn't the meaning of the words that mattered, anyway. It was the sound of them, the repetition, the very rhythm of the words themselves—our song, our ritual.

*

I've noticed that a barred owl, *Strix varia*, often called a "hoot owl," has taken up residence in the woods beyond my balcony. The line of trees separates my apartment building from the Wildwood Golf Club, and every once in a while, I'll hear shouts of "Fore!" or quick bursts of applause on a Sunday afternoon. At night, though, the woods become a forest; the golf course, a place where coyotes run free, sometimes howling when they've made a kill. I like to imagine those coyotes as stealthy hunters, and I believe, too, that my owl is healthier and plumper than the one housed at Natural Resources. That one doesn't call, not needing to because her mate can't break into the cage. I only know the owl from my woods is there because I hear his calls: "*Who cooks for you? Who cooks for you?*" I'm used to his sounds and I look forward to them. They're a part of the fabric of my life, now, something I can expect to hear when I'm grading papers or trying to name the constellations I can see between the trees. Barred owls like to stay put once

EVERY RIVER ON EARTH

they nest, but sometimes, they get restless. I've never seen my owl, and I likely never will, but if he leaves, I'll miss him all the same.

Dad jokes that someday I'll have to push him through the fairgrounds in a wheelchair. "You'll just have to cart me around," he says. "It'll make up for when I had to figure out how to keep you in the stroller." I tell him it's fine, that I'll be glad to, and then we say good-bye on the phone the way we always do, the decades of repeated words shaping the parameters of our relationship. What I haven't said is that Smokey and the giant slide wouldn't be the same without his stories. I'd miss his baseball hat and collection of State Fair pins, one for each year he's been. I don't tell him that I can't even imagine him in one of the rent-a-wheelchairs from the fair, or that I don't think I'll go without him. I haven't mentioned that to me, Dad is like that cement cardinal: a constant, changeless figure; one with flaws made invisible by year after year of bright new paint; one whose absence is so unimaginable it seems absurd.

caution: do not use with mono devices

This hillbilly stompbox of love
is only good in stereo, coming at you
from both sides, pulsing left to right.
Play me the shopping cart baby.
Be my *Einstürzende Neubauten* of the parking lot
while we load the groceries in the trunk.
This is not 1992, but I'm still hot for you.
I've found happiness in this sale on organic carrots
and the end of the season clearance on topsoil.
I've found happiness in the way the fog
circles these ridges, making Southern Ohio
look like Switzerland, clouds like mountains.

Swinging on the porch, reading *On the Road*,
watching the *Dendroica cerulean* eat and rest
on his way from Canada to the warm winter
of Belize. He is no Kerouac, knocking on doors
of empty basement apartments. This bird
would not call him wild, this bird would know
his antics by their scientific name:
Inconsidertia bullshitia.

Our quiet country night
is a bourgeois slavery?
Tie me up, tie me down, baby.
Just don't forget the safety word.

Moving to Adams County, 1973

Beside the road the creek sped
    over rocks, committed to the river
as we drove into nightfall, absorbed
    into the darkness along with the trees
that meshed above us.

The land fell steep and unruly,
    rumpling into hollows and hills
where the burley hung bronzing
    in open sheds as we left behind
the carved oak altar,

the linen napkins of Sundays.
    Here, richness lay in tangled plants,
wild fruit and the chance of snakes,
    and always the river ahead,
drawing us even as we stopped short of it,

A margin to honor, the edge
    of the place we had chosen
and would come to cherish
    as if nowhere else mattered,
and only then the knowledge

that we would not go at will,
    that we would be scissored
clean, freed to climb back
    into our old world,
the one we'd never truly find again.

JEAN MUSSER

Visiting Ohio

Crickets sing in the grass
over my father's ashes. At night
their sound wraps around me
in gentle rhythms like a string
section playing an adagio.

I feast with old friends.
We embrace and give toasts.
Like chaff, we are being winnowed
down to each other, some already
fragile as the glass-blown ships
that were sold at carnivals and fairs.

We ride down the wide river
in an open boat, glide under arches
of a limestone bridge built
before the Civil War. We joke
and tease each other. Mallards, grown
plump on algae, float in chevrons
ahead of us. A soft rain falls.

I have missed this lush green
midwestern heartland where everything
seems safe among rolling hills,
cities and towns with ample space.
Here and there still stand the homes
people assembled from Sears and Roebuck
catalogs after the First World War.

I visit a newly built Hospice home
with a large brick entryway shaped

like an embrace. Woods and streams,
gardens and waterfalls surround it.
In quiet private rooms, doors have been
opened for beds to be wheeled outside.
In the kitchen, a chef prepares lobster.

The living room resembles a fine hotel
with a grand player piano. Listening to
Mozart, I note with a chill how the keys
move although no one is there.

Tourist Brochure for Athens, Ohio

Round here, breaded chicken hearts will cost you $2.50 a box.

Round here, upright pianos can end up on the porch (too expensive to tune, too bulky of an animal).

Round here, a squirrel could once tree itself in Parkersburg, end up in Indiana, and never
touch the ground.

Round here, the pawpaw goes into homebrew, ice cream, salsas, even
has its own fall festival.

Round here, there's no train out. Not anymore. Bus leaves for Cincinnati
or Columbus.

Round here, the college lawns get unrivalled attention. No water or electric
just ten minutes down the road. Some folks play settlers, live that way
on purpose. Most? Oh, hell. No way.

Round here, we shine old mining towns into series of delis and meditation
rooms.
The last brick beehive kiln just got its first real crack.

Round here, new student condos went up on Shawnee burial grounds.
Front porches wear sloppy necklaces made of red party cups.

Round here, we got 270 cemeteries—some of 'em move. Just ask anybody
up there on Peach Ridge Road.

Round here, ghost-hunters stare right back at the crying angel statue or the
face of the devil
on a door in Wilson Hall. Spectral mist? We got it. Ghost-herd of bison?
A big draw.

Round here, the old asylum closed some twenty years back. And yet there's
movement
behind barred windows. We find a bit of lace out on the lawn.

Round here, you'd be committed for irregular bleeding, post-traumatic
fits, excessive
childbirth. Struck by lightning, even—in ya'd go.

Round here, still meet the patients who came on down the hill when all
that funding went

wonky in the '80s.

Round here, our children got two choices, mostly: get out, or get in uniform.
    Creeks slip down the mountains, orange ribbons full of acid. We already
        know
    that story: "little cities of black diamonds." We're workin' on a newer title.
        Yeah,
    we're workin' pretty hard.

Round here, we pronounce *Appalachia* any way we damn well please.

Caught Up in Summer

I'm sitting in the lap
of mother earth.
My daughter on the far
side of the country
looks for the Beats
of City Lights.
My husband, on the upside
of a hill, bales hay,
trying to outrace the storm.

Killing time, I root around
near the relics
of an old homestead.
I find plate shards:
white, trimmed in pale blue.
I pick up pieces of a crock
and wonder if the past
residents were pestered
by the same flies.

I feel those folks sitting here
shelling peas, peeling apples,
looking across the field of grass,
protected from wind and sun.

Me?
I'm hoping to stay out long enough
to get hit by lightning.

AUTHOR BIOGRAPHIES AND COMMENTARIES

DAVID BAKER is author of ten books of poetry, recently *Never-Ending Birds* (Norton, 2009), winner of the Theodore Roethke Memorial Poetry Prize, and four books of critical prose. He holds the Thomas B. Fordham Chair at Denison University, in Granville, Ohio, and is poetry editor of the *Kenyon Review*.

> *"My three poems, written over a span of many years, take place in southern and central Ohio from Granville to Gallipolis to the area south of Buckeye Lake. Each is a portrait of a person, a community, the wildlife, or landscape here where I've lived now for nearly thirty years."*

IVARS BALKITS received an Individual Artist Fellowship from the Ohio Arts Council in 1999. His works have been published in various literary magazines and anthologies, including *I Have My Own Song for It: Modern Poems of Ohio* (University of Akron Press, 2002).

> *"'Box' is a record of my impressions of the tiny structures abandoned in fields and woods in my part of southern Ohio. Fascinated with the decay and manner of falling apart of these many outbuildings, I thought also of those who might have once inhabited or used them."*

ROY BENTLEY has won awards from the NEA, the Florida Division of Cultural Affairs, and the Ohio Arts Council. *The Trouble with a Short Horse in Montana* won the White Pine Poetry Prize in 2005. *Starlight Taxi* won the 2012 Blue Lynx Prize for Poetry.

> *"I was born at Good Samaritan Hospital in Dayton. The people in these poems—my grandmother Bentley, Granny Potter, and my uncle Bill Potter— saw Montgomery County as a destination of both promise and possibility. Nonetheless, they carried home with them and seemed always to have one foot firmly planted, so to speak, across the Ohio River in their native Kentucky."*

DON BOGEN is the author of four books of poetry, most recently *An Algebra* (University of Chicago Press, 2009). Nathaniel Ropes Professor of English and Comparative Literature at the University of Cincinnati, he serves as poetry editor of the *Cincinnati Review*. His website is www.donbogen.com.

> "I suppose 'A Ride' is dated by the reference to videotape and the fact that our children are now adults, but its focus on the seemingly unchanging cycles along the Ohio River is still relevant. In 'Cardinals,' it seemed appropriate to capture the state bird's own daily cycles in haiku."

TANYA BOMSTA is currently a graduate student at Marshall University in West Virginia, where she studies English and teaches composition. She enjoys writing creative nonfiction and plans to pursue a doctoral degree in English.

> "Portsmouth, Ohio, is a small city located on the banks of the Ohio River. Portsmouth has its share of troubles, but it is a unique and memorable place that reflects the buoyant spirit of Appalachian Ohio. About that place, I offer this nonfiction work."

JEANNE BRYNER was born in Appalachia, and much of her writing deals with straddling two landscapes. She has received awards and fellowships for her fiction and poetry. A practicing registered nurse and author of seven books, she and her husband live near a dairy farm.

> "Appalachian Ohio reminds me of home: speech patterns of folks, rolling hills and winding roads, sheets drying on clotheslines and small towns peeking through spaces between weathered barns. The people who live in my poems and stories also live here mindful of rainfall and harvest. They still wave at strangers."

MICHELLE Y. BURKE is the author of the poetry chapbook *Horse Loquela*. Her poems have appeared in *Lake Effect*, *New Orleans Review*, *Hotel Amerika*, *Spoon River Poetry Review*, *Fiddleback*, *Waccamaw*, and elsewhere. She lives in Cincinnati.

> "I've done two stints of graduate school in Ohio. In order to stay sane while studying, I took horseback riding lessons and worked at a local farm. These poems come from those experiences."

A native Ohioan, CHRISTOPHER CITRO has a BA from Ohio University and an MFA from Indiana University. His poems have appeared in *Salamander*, *Cream City Review*, *Southeast Review*, *Poetry East*, the *Cincinnati*

Review, Verse Daily, and elsewhere. In 2006, he won the Langston Hughes Creative Writing Award for Poetry.

> "I first encountered the rolling hills of southeastern Ohio while a student in Athens. I return to the area often, visiting my brother's farm near the village of Scio (pop. 800) with its derelict pottery factory, and living and writing in an apartment above Main Street there in 2011."

ED DAVIS is the author of the novels *I Was So Much Older Then* (Disc-Us Books, 2001) and *The Measure of Everything* (Plain View Press, 2005), as well as many published stories and poems. He lives in the village of Yellow Springs, Ohio, where he bikes, hikes, blogs, and meditates.

> "Food, religion, extended family, insiders and outsiders, and a surprising offer from a desperate widower: I tried to create a boiling Appalachian stew in this chapter from a novel in progress."

CATHRYN ESSINGER is the author of three volumes of poetry—*A Desk in the Elephant House, My Dog Does Not Read Plato,* and *What I Know about Innocence.* She is a member of the Greenville Poets and a retired professor of English. She is currently teaching poetry workshops at the Antioch Writers Workshop and at Wright State University.

> "I've always loved the natural landscape of Appalachian Ohio, especially those intersections where towns and farmland lead into woods and creek beds—those 'just around the corner' places that are mostly hidden even from the country roads. In these poems, I talk to nature, and sometimes, if I'm lucky, she talks back in a magical sort of way."

The poems of DAVID LEE GARRISON have appeared in *Connecticut Review, Poem,* and *Rattle;* they have also been read on *The Writer's Almanac* by Garrison Keillor and featured by Ted Kooser on *American Life in Poetry.* His new book is *Playing Bach in the DC Metro.*

> "My grandmother grew up in the Baptist tradition of southern Ohio, and 'Folding Tables and Five-Card Stud' stems from memories of her and stories she told me. In 'Every River on Earth,' the Amish tradition provides the starting point for some reflections on time. 'Route 4' resulted from a trip I took from Dayton to Sandusky on that two-lane highway. If Ohio is 'the heart of it all,' Route 4 is the aorta."

RON D. GILES was raised in New Boston, Ohio. During his career in television, he was awarded seven regional Emmys and was part of the original QVC management team. With three books under his belt, he is working on a fourth. Ron is a baritone soloist, a Kentucky Colonel, and has a Star on the Portsmouth Floodwall.

> "It is 1955, in New Boston, Ohio. The Detroit Steel mill is pumping prosperity into the region. Teenagers from all around drive polished cars with lancer hubcaps and curb feelers to the Steelworker's Hall on Gallia Street to bop and stroll at the Friday night dance. An inexperienced thirteen-year-old boy, who can't bop, is there as well in this nonfiction piece."

BENJAMIN S. GROSSBERG's books are *Space Traveler* (University of Tampa Press, 2014); *Sweet Core Orchard* (University of Tampa Press, 2009), winner of the 2008 Tampa Review Prize and a Lambda Literary Award; and *Underwater Lengths in a Single Breath* (Ashland Poetry Press, 2007).

> "These poems follow my move from a Yellow Springs apartment to a small farm, where I planted an orchard. Taken together, they suggest why Ohio displaced New Jersey—where I was born—as the place where I say I'm from: the fellowship I found there with the people and landscape."

RICHARD HAGUE has lived in Ohio all his life. Of his fourteen books, the most recent of which is *Learning How: Stories, Yarns & Tales* (Bottom Dog Press, 2011), many are set in eastern and southern Ohio. *Alive in Hard Country* was the 2003 Poetry Book of the Year of the Appalachian Writers Association.

> "Along the waterways of southern Ohio, the sycamore is the most striking tree, often leaning far out over the water, its thick roots gripping the bank. The following nonfiction was prompted by sycamores, which may be the largest living things in Ohio. Wherever, they are a wonder. Even in the city."

MICHAEL HENSON's collection of stories *The Way the World Is: The Maggie Boylan Stories* recently won the Brighthorse Prize in short fiction. This collection, which includes "Coming Home," is to be published by Brighthorse Books. Henson is author of three previous books of fiction and four collections of poetry. He lives in Cincinnati.

> "Appalachian Ohio has been hit hard with an epidemic of opiate addiction. OxyContin, methadone, heroin, and other chemicals have wrecked lives in both

urban and rural parts of the region. This fictional story tells of one woman's start at a rocky recovery."

A recent Wright State University graduate, HAYLEY HUGHES has participated in numerous professional creative nonfiction workshops and conferences across the country. She's been published in the *Fogdog Review, Cobalt,* the *Eunoia Review,* and *Proteus.* Hayley's essay "Filling the Void" was recently nominated for the 2012 *Best of the Net Anthology.*

"This nonfiction, 'The Fair,' explores how annual trips to the Ohio State Fair shaped how I perceive summer, but on a deeper level, attempts to explain my feelings about the Midwest itself as someone who deeply loves the place she comes from while also feeling compelled to leave."

Originally from Zanesville, Ohio, MARK ALLEN JENKINS completed an MFA at Bowling Green State University and is currently a PhD student at the University of Texas at Dallas, where he serves as assistant editor for *Reunion: The Dallas Review.* His poetry has appeared in *Memorious, Shot Glass Journal, Muse & Stone, Wild Goose Poetry Review,* and elsewhere.

"Living away from Zanesville for nearly ten years makes me appreciate its varied history more than when I lived there, and like James Wright, I've started to write about it from afar with a mixture of empathy and nostalgia."

CHRISTINA JONES is an MA candidate at Ohio University in Athens, Ohio, studying English/creative fiction writing. She received her BA in English at Shawnee State University in Portsmouth, Ohio. She has been previously published in journals such as *Rubbertop Review, Quarter After,* and Shawnee State University's *Silhouette* and *Tapestries.*

"Inspired by the beauty of the natural surroundings and the harsh oppression of a failing economy, this fictional story, 'The Last Shot,' tells of a southern Ohio man who encapsulates a culture of people struggling between life-altering moral choices and survival on a daily basis."

JENNIFER SCHOMBURG KANKE is a PhD candidate in English at Florida State University. Her work has appeared or is forthcoming in *Pleiades,* the *Laurel Review,* and *Fugue.* Formerly an editor of *Quarter after Eight,* she currently serves as poetry editor for the *Southeast Review.*

"*Even though I grew up in Columbus, the hills always seemed like home. When I moved to Athens County in 1993, I thought it was a temporary thing. Seventeen years and thirteen acres later, this poem was born.*"

DIANE KENDIG's latest chapbook is *The Places We Find Ourselves*. Previous poetry chapbooks include *A Tunnel of Flute Song* and *Greatest Hits 1978–2000*. Recently her poems have appeared in anthologies by New York University, Mayapple, Red Hen, and Bottom Dog Presses. You can find out more about her work at dianekendig.com.

"*I am indebted for this poem to Jim Gorman, who, leading a workshop at the 1999 James Wright Festival, pointed us to Wright's 'Written on a Big Cheap Postcard from Verona' and handed us . . . a big cheap postcard space to write in.*"

REBECCA J. R. LACHMAN teaches and tutors writing at Ohio University. She is a grateful graduate of the Bennington Writing Seminars (MFA) and the Ohio University Creative Writing Department (MA). Her first book of poems, *The Apple Speaks*, is available from Cascadia Publishing House.

"*I only discovered the unadulterated version of Athens, Ohio, after marrying an 'Athenian' after graduate school. Having lived here for nearly a decade, I am constantly amazed by the area's identity, historical clout, and overall hutzpah. 'Tourist Brochure for Athens, Ohio' personifies the Appalachian foothills/party school/ghost-hunting hotspot/locavore city as speaker.*"

When JANET LADRACH retired from teaching, she focused on poetry. She won 1st–3rd places in Ohio Poetry Day Contests and was published in *We'Moon*, a datebook of women's art and writing. A featured reader at Tim Horton's in Coshocton, she is also the new secretary for the Ohio Poetry Association.

"*Farming has long been a part of Appalachian Ohio culture. For those chosen by it, there is no other life. It affects relationships and molds people into a distinct lifestyle. The remoteness can cause feelings of isolation and people look for some kind of relief.*"

CATHY CULTICE LENTES is a poet, essayist, and children's writer. Her work has appeared in journals such as *Now & Then*, *Riverwind*, and *Blueline*, as well as in anthologies such as *I Have My Own Song for It: Modern Poems of Ohio* (University of Akron Press, 2002).

> "The poem was written for my son who was going to college and working in Cleveland, so far away from the green hills of home. He kept a copy of the poem on his refrigerator as a reminder that he was (and is) always connected to the things he loves."

SUE LONNEY writes to understand what she thinks. Coming from the Northwest to southern Ohio, where everyone is a poet and every object a poem, she joined a poetry group and learned from its members. She's old, not so wise, but still writes now and then.

> "In southern Ohio the hills pulse with a low beat. On foggy mornings, if you stand still with just a cup of coffee in your hand, you can see them move. Mountains are too big and flat areas just lie there. But Ohio hills have a way of shifting . . ."

HERBERT WOODWARD MARTIN has published eight volumes of poems. He has devoted over three decades to reading, editing, and performing the works of Paul Laurence Dunbar. He has received four honorary degrees for his scholarship on the poet. He is Professor Emeritus of English from the University of Dayton.

> "In the fall of 2001, I was visiting Professor of Creative Writing at Shawnee State University. I asked my students to write about a personage or an event from the town. I chose Kathleen Battle. The poem questions the origins of her talent. Is talent inherited, taught, in the water, air, streets and woods?"

PRESTON MARTIN received a Bachelor of General Studies from Ohio University and an MAT from the College of Charleston, SC. He is a retired teacher who still teaches, and writes.

> "Both sides of my family were born and raised in Appalachian Ohio. All childhood summers and most holidays were spent in and around Adams County, where the hills and fields and farms, and endless family stories, offered a wonderful education of the ways of the world."

JULIE L. MOORE is the author of *Slipping Out of Bloom* (WordTech Editions) and *Election Day* (Finishing Line Press). She lives in Cedarville, Ohio, with her family and is the writing center director at Cedarville University. You can learn more about her poetry at www.julielmoore.com.

"Having grown up in south Jersey, I am sometimes considered an outsider in southern Ohio, yet I feel right at home. 'A Clear Path' and 'The Poet Performs in the Theatre of Cows' use humor to explore how this rural landscape, where I've lived since 1987, intrigues and sustains me."

JEAN MUSSER is a poet and playwright whose first book of poetry, *The Crimson Hat*, was published in 2011. Originally from Akron, she graduated from Case Western Reserve, and later became art critic for the *Seattle Times*. Her poems appear in *Brilliant Corners*, *Interdisciplinary Studies*, *Raven Chronicles*, and *PoetsWest Literary Journal*.

"Both poems portray occasions for emotional bonding. 'Ohio Lightning' recounts a physical and emotional storm that brought me closer to my parents, while in 'Visiting Ohio' a college reunion brings a confluence of loss and camaraderie ending with a ghostly piano playing. These poetic images help in our healing."

JOEL PECKHAM is the author of three poetry collections, *Movers and Shakers*, *The Heat of What Comes*, and *Nightwalking*. Recently Academy Chicago Publishers released his memoir, *Resisting Elegy*. Poems have appeared in *Black Warrior Review*, *Prairie Schooner*, the *Southern Review*, and elsewhere. He lives with his family in Huntington, West Virginia.

"I work at a branch campus of UC that sits twenty minutes north of Kentucky. When the economy went south a few years ago, it hit our district as hard as any in the country. 'Everything Must Go' is a response to the foreclosure crisis. 'Psalm 96' is really a celebratory ode to my students—the single moms, the unemployed factory workers, the vets coming home from Afghanistan. I love them dearly."

DONALD RAY POLLOCK grew up in Knockemstiff, Ohio, and worked at a paper mill in nearby Chillicothe for over thirty-two years. His first book, a collection of short stories called *Knockemstiff*, won the PEN/Robert Bingham Fellowship; and his second book, a novel called *The Devil All the Time*, was voted one of the ten best books of 2011 by *Publishers Weekly*.

"Originally, this story was going to be about being outside the Lucasville Prison the night Wendell Berry was executed in February 1999, which shows how much an idea can morph over time. On the way home that night, I saw a nativity scene still on display in someone's yard, hence the title."

BROOKS REXROAT teaches writing in Cincinnati. He holds an MFA in creative writing from Southern Illinois University, and his work has appeared in the *Cleveland Review, Weave Magazine, Revolution House, Midwestern Gothic*, and the *Montreal Review*. Visit him online at http://brooksrexroat.com.

"*Born and raised in Appalachian Ohio, I've spent a great deal of time in and near river towns, several of which were also single-industry cities. New Boston, Ohio, exemplifies both. This story is set in a fictionalized version of that town, where an incident involving the remains of a shuttered steel mill reshapes the narrator's relationship with his hometown.*"

BRIAN RICHARDS lives in a small cabin, sans electricity or phone, on a ridge overlooking the Ohio River Valley. He is the author of a number of books of poetry, most recently *Enridged*, from the University of New Orleans Press.

"*These pieces are concerned with making sense of what I see. Only experience is sensitive.*"

ADAM SOL is the author of three books of poetry, including *Jeremiah, Ohio*, a novel in poems, which was shortlisted for Ontario's Trillium Award for Poetry; and *Crowd of Sounds*, which won the award in 2004. He teaches at Laurentian University's campus in Barrie, Ontario, and lives in Toronto.

"*I lived in Cincinnati for a number of years, taught a bit in Batavia, and wandered a lot in my car. When you're driving and have hundreds of fleeting impressions and images, it's hard to organize them with any coherence. This poem was one small way that I tried to do that.*"

LIANNE SPIDEL grew up in Detroit, graduated from Wittenberg University and the University of Michigan, taught high school for thirty-one years, and is a member of the Greenville Poets, Greenville, Ohio. Chapbooks: *Chrome* (Finishing Line Press, 2006); *What to Tell Joseme* (Main Street Rag, 2011); *Pairings*, poetry and art by Ann Loveland (Dos Madres Press, 2012).

"*Moving to Appalachian Ohio with my family was a shock. Some of my students had never been out of Adams County, but its people could do anything—the* most creative, unspoiled people I ever knew. My boys grew up there. We left, but in many ways it still contains us."

MYRNA STONE is the author of three books of poems, *The Casanova Chronicles*, *How Else to Love the World*, and *The Art of Loss*. Her poems have appeared in such journals as *Poetry*, *Ploughshares*, and *TriQuarterly*, and in seven anthologies. She is a founding member of the Greenville Poets.

"These poems are based on memories of growing up in small-town Versailles, in the heart of farm country in southern Ohio. Did we really burn down barns? Or did we only want to? And where did innocence go that day my little friend and I played dress-up?"

SCOTT URBAN's prose, poetry, and reviews have appeared in numerous print and electronic publications. Recent poems have appeared in *Word Salad*, *Cairn*, and *Cyclamens and Swords*. His poetry collections include *Night's Voice*, *Skull-Job*, and *Alight*. He teaches at Nelsonville's Hocking College in Athens County.

"In the summer of 2011, my family relocated to southern Ohio after living for more than twenty years on North Carolina's Cape Fear Coast. As I explored my new home, I was entranced by the area's deep primeval forests, its serpentine county roads, and its secluded glens harboring mist into the afternoon. Poems drenched in an Ohio atmosphere began to spill out of my pen, some of them colored by autumn and tinged with melancholy, including this one."

MICHAEL WATERSON was born in Pittsburgh, Pennsylvania, and lives in Napa, California. Mike received a BA in Creative Writing from San Francisco State University and an MFA from Mills College. He was Napa Valley Poet Laureate 2010–11. He works as an editor for Napa Valley Publishing.

"Born a little way upriver from him, I have always loved James Wright's poetry. Li Po, who appears in Wright's work, was a famous poet of the Tang dynasty. Legend says he was a great drunkard and drowned trying to embrace a reflection of the moon in the river."

LAURA MADELINE WISEMAN has a doctorate from the University of Nebraska–Lincoln, where she teaches English. She is the author of six collections of poetry, including *Sprung* (San Francisco Bay Press, 2012), *Farm Hands* (Gold Quoin Press, 2012), and *She Who Loves Her Father* (Dancing Girl Press, 2012). www.lauramadelinewiseman.com

"These poems were written from my experiences of growing up in the Midwest. I was born in Iowa; my adolescence was in Iowa and my childhood in southern Ohio. I have family all over the Buckeye State. These poems were written with that Ohio childhood and family in mind."

DALLAS WOODBURN's work has appeared in *Arcadia Journal, Monkeybicycle*, and the *Los Angeles Times*. Recent awards include the Ninth Glass Woman Prize, the Brian Mexicott Playwriting Award, and a nomination for the Pushcart Prize. She teaches undergraduate writing courses at Purdue University and is fiction editor of *Sycamore Review*. www.writeonbooks.org

"Though I grew up in California, my family originally hails from small-town Appalachian Ohio, and I spent many childhood summers there. It is a place I find myself returning to again and again, as here, in my fiction."

BEVERLY ZEIMER, whose poems celebrate life in southern rural Ohio, is the daughter of tenant farmers. The winner of a Pudding House chapbook competition, she was nominated by publisher Jennifer Bosveld for the Pushcart Prize. She shares her work as a featured reader at coffeehouses, poetry events, and festivals throughout Ohio.

"During hunting season, when Daddy went to the backfields to feed the cattle, he took his guns—a 12-gauge shotgun and his trusty twenty-two—to a wooded area near Deer Creek, where Mommy, one day, determined to break Grandma of smoking, threw her precious tobacco pipe into the rushing water."

PERMISSIONS

David Baker: "Outside" is reprinted from *The Southern Review* with permission of the author. "Patriotics," from *Sweet Home, Saturday Night*. Copyright 1991 by David Baker. Reprinted with the permission of The Permissions Company, Inc., on behalf of the University of Arkansas Press, www.uapress .com. "Too Many," from *Never-Ending Birds* by David Baker. Copyright 2009 by David Baker. Used by permission of W.W. Norton & Company, Ince.

Don Bogen: "A Ride," from *The Known World*, copyright 1997 by Don Bogen. Reprinted by permission of Wesleyan University Press. "Cardinals," from *Luster*, copyright 2003 by Don Bogen. Reprinted by permission of Wesleyan University Press.

Michelle Y. Burke: "Horse Loquela" first appeared in *Horse Loquela, Red Mountain Review*, 2007. Reprinted by permission of the author. "Market Day," from Dorothy Sargent Rosenberg Poetry Prizes, 2011, Dorothyprizes .org. Reprinted by permission of the author.

Christopher Citro: "In This Reality, You Exit at the Next McDonald's for Fries and a Shake" first appeared in the *Cincinnati Review*. Reprinted by permission of the author.

David Lee Garrison: "Every River on Earth," from *Playing Bach in the D.C. Metro*, copyright 2012 by David Lee Garrison. Reprinted by permission of Browser Books Publishing. "Folding Tables and Five-Card Stud" and "Route 4," from *Sweeping the Cemetery*, copyright 2007 by David Lee Garrison. Reprinted by permission of Browser Books Publishing.

Ronald D. Giles: "The Friday Night Dance," from *On Harrisonville Avenue*, copyright 2008 by Ronald D. Giles. Reprinted by permission of the author.

Benjamin S. Grossberg: "In Memoriam: Ginger" and "Not Children," from *Sweet Core Orchard*, copyright 2009 by Benjamin S. Grossberg. Reprinted by permission of University of Tampa Press.

DISCUSSION QUESTIONS

I. FAMILY AND FOLKS

1. In this first section, the writers often express a strong emotional bond with family members. With which individual pieces could you most relate? Which pieces did you find most moving?

2. The speakers in various pieces convey definite views about community and neighborliness. Which selections most stimulated your own thoughts on the subject? Which selections struck you as particularly insightful, authentic, or universal?

II. THE LAND

1. Nature and land play influential roles in the identity of Appalachian Ohio. In what ways does the land function in relation to the people? Can Nature be considered its own character?

2. What specific forms of life—plant, animal, the elements, and so on—dominate in this selection of writings as things of beauty, things that haunt, and things that help define Appalachian Ohio?

III. THE GRIND

1. Certain hardships for the people in this region seem almost emblematic. How do the writers convey possible reasons for these specific struggles? Which selections most inspire hope? Which selections provide the best insight into possible solutions?

2. Hardships are present in the lives of Appalachian Ohioans. In what ways do people respond to suffering?

IV. HOME AND AWAY

1. In this section, memory often works as a tool for the writers and their characters. How is memory used for emotional exploration and self-identity? How do distance and time provide insight, distortion, and sometimes a new sense of self?

2. Which selections best capture a sense of place for you as a reader? How do the writers achieve this effect?

MISCELLANEOUS

1. Based on the entire range of literary selections in this collection, what are the stylistic tendencies that the writers and poets share? Could these tendencies indicate anything about being a writer/poet of Appalachian Ohio?

2. Characterize the humor that exists in selections for which you can detect a sense of humor. How does the narrator, or a character, or a situation create humor in these pieces?

3. Based on this collection's various selections, how do the experiences of men and women in Appalachian Ohio differ?

4. After reading this collection, what do you think you would most enjoy about living in Appalachian Ohio? What would you least enjoy—and maybe even fear?

5. Which are your favorite selections in each section? Why? Which appeal to you the least? Why?

6. Which poem do you think best captures the spirit of the region? Which story?

7. What would you write about to add to this collection? Would your piece be best conceived as a poem, essay, or story?

8. Is there an overall mood created by the selections in *Every River on Earth*? If not, what are the prevailing moods?

9. What impression does the cover photo create for you? If you were to choose an image to evoke Appalachian Ohio to put on the cover, what would it be?

10. Choose three contributors whose pieces intrigue you. What questions would you ask them about their pieces?

ABOUT THE EDITOR

Neil Carpathios is the author of eight poetry collections, most recently: *Playground of Flesh* (Main Street Rag Publishing Company, 2006), *At the Axis of Imponderables* (winner of the Quercus Review Press Book Award, 2007), and *Beyond the Bones* (FutureCycle Press, 2009). His newspaper column, "Let's Talk Poetry," appears weekly in the *Portsmouth Daily Times* and strives to showcase the works of various poets, especially those living in Appalachian Ohio. He teaches at Shawnee State University, where he also serves as Coordinator of Creative Writing.